"With an encyclopedic knowledge unfo. a beautiful, soigné text, Veronica Mary time and vividly inhabit Julian's fourteen remarkable life and writings. Rolf's guid _. when we re- luctantly return to our equally troubled tw....y-first century, Julian travels with us and intimately inhabits and transforms our world and outlook. Stunning, unforgettable, and life changing."

David Wilbourne, honorary assistant bishop in the Diocese of York

"Veronica Mary Rolf skillfully reveals the historical significance and contemporary relevance of Julian of Norwich. In our renewed interest in the writings of Christian spirituality, Lady Julian can instruct us in the centrality of the Trinity, the nature of sin and grace, God's providence, and suffering and prayer. Rolf serves as a wise and gentle guide to illuminate both first time and seasoned readers. This book is deeply learned and highly practical."

Tom Schwanda, associate professor of Christian formation and ministry at Wheaton College

"Julian of Norwich is an underappreciated gem—she belongs alongside Augustine and Aquinas as one of the greatest of Christian spiritual guides. Thanks to Veronica Mary Rolf, the life and teachings of this great mystic are more accessible than ever. *An Explorer's Guide to Julian of Norwich* offers a clear and insightful introduction to Julian, one of the treasures of our faith."

Carl McColman, author of *Befriending Silence* and *Answering the Contemplative Call*

"Rolf's work is more than an informative guide by an expert in Julian scholarship. The reader begins to feel the heartbeat of this great mystic as the author works around key texts and highlights choice quotations. This could only have come from someone who is intimately acquainted with her. Whether one is a first-time or seasoned explorer, this book will not disappoint."

Simon Chan, Trinity Theological College, Singapore

"Taking on the role of tour guide, Veronica Mary Rolf leads us on an engaging, vivid, and historically rich journey with Julian of Norwich. A figure both familiar and mystifying, Julian comes into view with gentle clarity through Rolf's accessible and deeply researched voice. I highly recommend this book to spiritual seekers, retreat leaders, and scholars alike."

Jennifer Davidson, American Baptist Seminary of the West, Graduate Theological Union

"Julian of Norwich is among the most radiant of Christian mystics. The radiance is all the brighter for Julian's frankness in questioning the darkness she experienced in her culture and in herself in a deeply troubled time. The unequivocal and insatiable love of God for all his creatures rings in her words throughout her book. Veronica Mary Rolf is a scholar with a deep heart that probes the mysteries Julian probes and uses her historical and textual research to shed clarity and light on Julian's teaching that speaks to our own time with increasing urgency."

Andrew Marr, OSB, author of *Moving and Resting in God's Desire*, abbot of St. Gregory's Abbey in Three Rivers, MI

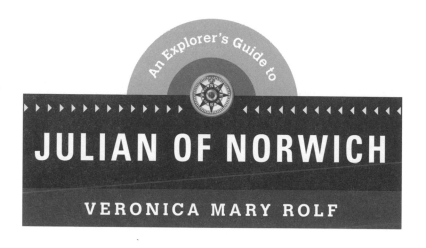

An Explorer's Guide to

JULIAN OF NORWICH

VERONICA MARY ROLF

IVP Academic

An imprint of InterVarsity Press
Downers Grove, Illinois

InterVarsity Press
P.O. Box 1400, Downers Grove, IL 60515-1426
ivpress.com
email@ivpress.com

InterVarsity Press® is the book-publishing division of InterVarsity Christian Fellowship/USA®, a movement of students and faculty active on campus at hundreds of universities, colleges, and schools of nursing in the United States of America, and a member movement of the International Fellowship of Evangelical Students. For information about local and regional activities, visit intervarsity.org.

Scripture quotations, unless otherwise noted, are from the New Revised Standard Version of the Bible, copyright 1989 by the Division of Christian Education of the National Council of the Churches of Christ in the USA. Used by permission. All rights reserved.

Translations of Julian's Revelations are the author's and are taken from Veronica Mary Rolf, Julian's Gospel: Illuminating the Life & Revelations of Julian of Norwich (Maryknoll, NY: Orbis Books, 2013). Used by permission.

Figures 3.1, 3.2, 3.3, and 3.4 are used with the kind permission of The Friends of Julian of Norwich.

Figure 4.1 is an excerpt of Julian of Norwich's Long Text. Used by permission of Bibliothèque nationale de France.

Cover design: David Fassett
Interior design: Beth McGill
Images: gold compass: ©RUSSELLTATEdotCOM/iStockphoto
writing: Description of Julian's illness and vision in 1373, from 'The Beginning of Julian's Spiritual Vision, in a Collection of Theological Works, including Julian of Norwich,' 1450 (ink & colour on vellum), English School, (15th century) / British Library, London, UK / © British Library Board. All Rights Reserved / Bridgeman Images
portrait: Portrait of a Young Woman by Rogier van der Weyden at Gemäldegalerie Picture Gallery, Berlin / Wikimedia Commons

ISBN 978-0-8308-5088-4 (print)
ISBN 978-0-8308-8737-8 (digital)

Printed in the United States of America ∞

InterVarsity Press is committed to ecological stewardship and to the conservation of natural resources in all our operations. This book was printed using sustainably sourced paper.

Library of Congress Cataloging-in-Publication Data
A catalog record for this book is available from the Library of Congress.

P	20	19	18	17	16	15	14	13	12	11	10	9	8	7	6	5	4	3	2	1
Y	35	34	33	32	31	30	29	28	27	26	25	24	23	22	21	20	19	18

In loving memory of

Beatrice Brennan, RSCJ,

a woman of profound faith,

probing intellect,

and boundless compassion,

who first spoke Julian's

words to me.

And for all those who dare

to hope that *alle shalle be wele*

because God is love.

Contents

A Note on Citations

My primary textual source has been the critical edition by Nicholas Watson and Jacqueline Jenkins, *The Writings of Julian of Norwich: A Vision Showed to a Devout Woman and A Revelation of Love* (University Park: Pennsylvania State University Press, 2006). In making my own translation of Julian's Middle English, I chose to retain spellings of some of her favorite words to evoke the distinctive sound of her voice on the page. Sometimes I have restructured the syntax slightly and inserted a few extra words, but only when necessary for comprehension. For readers wishing to compare my translation with the original Middle English in Watson and Jenkins, I have cited chapter numbers referring to Julian's Short Text (*A Vision*) in Roman numerals. In referencing Julian's Long Text (*A Revelation*), I have listed chapter numbers in Arabic numbers.

Julian refers repeatedly to God as "he," and she uses the terms "man" or "mankind" (or Adam) as being inclusive of all men *and women*. Occasionally she writes "a man and a woman," which, given the dominant male culture, was most unusual. However, since it would have been anachronistic (and unfaithful to the text) to render all of Julian's references gender-neutral, I beg the reader's understanding: she used the language available to her. It reflects her culture, not her bias. Indeed, Julian will dare to speak of Christ as Mother.

Preface

Julian of Norwich is one of the best and least known women in medieval history. New translations of her extraordinary work, *The Revelations of Divine Love*, emerge on a seasonal basis and are studied side by side with Chaucer's *Canterbury Tales* in medieval literature and interpretive theory courses, both at the undergraduate and graduate levels. Her theological insights and spiritual direction are compared to those of St. Teresa of Avila and St. John of the Cross. Julian's writings have become essential reading in any survey of the development of Western Christian mysticism, medieval theology, and postmodern feminism. Her Long Text continues to provide a rich field for graduate theses and PhD dissertations in religious studies departments. Julian's *Revelations* have been translated from Middle English into many languages; thus her readership is worldwide. There is an Episcopalian Order of Julian of Norwich in the United States for nuns and monks and Julian meditation groups for Anglicans in England. Her appeal extends to every Christian denomination and beyond: to Jews, Buddhists, and Muslims, as well as agnostics and atheists. It seems there is something for everyone in Julian's writings.

On the more popular front, there are books of Julian spirituality, collections of her "sayings," meditation manuals, poetry and musical compositions, paintings and sculptures, television documentaries, novelistic treatments, and stage plays. I fully expect a "Julian app" on your phone any day now with a Julian quote to wake you up every morning. Her soaring popularity would be the envy of any political candidate. Moreover, every year thousands of tourists make a pilgrimage to Julian's reconstructed anchorage in Norwich, England, to sit and pray where Julian herself sat and prayed. Perhaps they also come to wonder: What would make a woman choose to be permanently enclosed in a one-room cloister for some twenty-five years in order to devote her life to prayer, contemplation, and the writing of her *Revelations*? Julian's very strangeness may be what attracts us; she is like no other historical figure we have ever met.

Does all this buzz actually enable us to hear the voice of Julian of Norwich? Does it help us get closer to this fascinating woman and her inspired text? Admittedly, something valuable is gained through the phenomenon of popular awareness. People of all ages and cultural backgrounds feel encouraged to look to Julian for guidance in their daily struggles, consult Julian's *Revelations* with their questions and doubts, and seek guidance from Julian in their spiritual crises. And this is all to the good.

But something is also lost by the proliferation of "Juliana." As with other postmodern trends, Julian the mystic, the seeker, the theologian, and the ardent lover of Jesus Christ, is in danger of becoming just one more popular saint, a passing fad, a talis*woman*, or perhaps the prophet of instant consolation. Her most famous words—"All shall be well"—are printed on greeting cards and coffee cups, carved on plaques, necklaces, bracelets, even fashioned into tattoos. This profound "saying" has become many people's sole connection to Julian. However, it is often misunderstood as an immediate feel-good panacea for all our trials and troubles, and that is not its true meaning at all. Herein lies the danger of a too-facile, too-succinct summing up of a major mystical theologian with a single sentence. The full range of Julian's groundbreaking theology can be submerged by her popular appeal. Julian has so much more to say to us!

Still, for those determined to embark on a voyage into the vast riches of Julian's writings, there remains a real problem. After all, Julian lived in the fourteenth century, perhaps the most tumultuous century in history (next to the twentieth), and she was far removed from our way of living, writing, and thinking. Furthermore, she wrote in a still-unformed vernacular (termed "Middle English" by linguistic scholars), a language that had no consistent spelling or rules of grammar. Even Julian's contemporary Geoffrey Chaucer had to create his own written language. But Chaucer was well-educated; Julian was not. She had to make up the language, and her unique way of expressing complex theological ideas, as she went along. In essence, Julian's writing was her way of speaking, of conversing intimately with her readers, whom she called her *evencristens* (fellow Christians). Her language is shot through with startling images, rich metaphors, intellectual brilliance, sudden flashes of insight, high energy, prayerful reflection, bouts of fear, deeply-rooted faith, and most of all, a passionate love of God.

Yet such "spoken" language can be extremely difficult for a contemporary reader to fathom, especially when reading from the original text with unfamiliar spelling. When first approaching Julian's *Revelations*, you may have trouble entering into her medieval mindset. You may be thoroughly mystified by her mystical theology. You may become impatient with her reflective method of weaving round and round a topic, ruminating on the *Revelations* over and over again until they become clearer—to her as well as to her readers. You may not agree with her conviction that there is "no wrath in God," that there is a "godly will" at the core of everyone's being. You may not relate easily to her theology of the motherhood of God. You may not comprehend the Christological import of her parable of the lord and the servant. You may find Julian by turns appealing, shocking, challenging, and profoundly life-changing. You will never find Julian dull.

These are a few of the common experiences of a first encounter with Julian's *Revelations*, or even of multiple encounters. Unless you have a guide to help you learn how to read and *hear* Julian—so that her voice "speaks" to you right off the page—you might get stuck on a complex sentence or a theological concept and be tempted to give up. And that would be a great loss.

Just as a traveler benefits greatly from a tour guide in a foreign country—a guide who knows the history and culture of the land, and understands the nuances of the spoken language—so an explorer into the unfamiliar world of Julian of Norwich may have the trip made much smoother by a personal guide. I hope to be just such a guide for you. I will lead you into the historical and theological context of Julian's text in order to shed light on the deeper meanings hidden within the *Revelations*. And once I give you key insights into Julian's writings, you will more easily identify with her spiritual conflicts, her courageous faith, her hard-won hope, and most of all, her profound realization that ultimately, because God is love, "alle shalle be wele."

I have divided our journey into two parts. In part one, "Getting to Know Julian of Norwich," I will ask "Why Julian Now?" and start by sharing how I came to know and love Julian, and what led me to spend many years researching and writing my previous book, *Julian's Gospel*. I will begin relating Julian's story, discuss the "three gifts" she desired in her youth, describe her near-death experience, and introduce you to her as the mystic, the seeker, and the theologian. I will also suggest why a woman who lived and wrote over six hundred years ago is worth reading today, and why her visionary experiences and theological insights are directly relevant to our totally different lives in the twenty-first century.

In order to discover the woman behind the text, I will explore what we can know about Julian's history from the cataclysmic events that directly affected her life in the fourteenth century, as well as from clues in her text. Thereafter, I will pose and answer some intriguing questions about Julian and engage in some lively myth-busting. I will also provide information about the fascinating history of Julian's texts and their near destruction through the centuries. Then I will present a glossary of Julian's favorite terms to help you learn a little Middle English—at least enough to find your way around Julian's text. With all this pre-departure information, your bags will be well-packed and you will be ready to embark on a pilgrimage into the world of Julian's *Revelations*.

In part two, "Exploring the *Revelations of Divine Love*," I will take you on a guided tour of Julian's *Revelations*, pausing now and then to suggest the relevance of Julian's insights for our lives. In the next chapter, "Digging Deeper into Julian's Themes," we will explore some further implications of Julian's theological insights such as trinitarian *oneing*, "no wrath or blame in God," "alle shalle be wele," the parable of the lord and the servant, and the ground of being. Thereafter, to highlight the distinctly *spiritual* dimension of our pilgrimage, I will share some helpful guidelines for making (or leading) a retreat with Julian's *Revelations* based on this guidebook and my own years of experience in leading such retreats. Finally, in the last chapter, I will suggest resources for further exploration and study.

Now that we have our itinerary all set, we're ready to begin our pilgrimage!

Acknowledgments

No one works alone. As I research and write, I am surrounded by the presence of those "holy angels" who have loved and believed in me throughout my life: grandparents, parents, relatives, teachers, friends, spiritual guides, spouse, children, and grandchildren. I give thanks with all my heart for my parents, Veronica and Edward, who persisted through great hardships and with tremendous love to give their three children all the opportunities they themselves never had. I also want to acknowledge the professors and mentors who nourished my passion for theology, literature, medieval studies, historical research, the dramatic arts, and creative writing.

I am continually grateful for my dear friends, whose love and laughter, intellectual stimulation, and emotional encouragement are a source of great blessing. I also wish to thank the numerous colleagues with whom I have worked throughout my decades in the professional theatre, as well as for the hundreds of students—of both theatre arts and the history of Christian mysticism—whom I have been privileged to teach in the United States and abroad. You have enriched my life and taught *me* in countless ways.

During my many years of research on Julian of Norwich, I have been guided by the critical editions of Julian's *Revelations* by Edmund Colledge, OSA, and James Walsh, SJ; Georgia Ronan Crampton; and Nicholas Watson and Jacqueline Jenkins. In addition, I am deeply indebted to the superb scholarship of Caroline Walker Bynum, Margaret Deanesly, Eamon Duffy, Katherine L. French, Kerrie Hide, Grace M. Jantzen, Bernard McGinn, May McKisack, Joan M. Nuth, Margaret Ann Palliser, Shulamith Shahar, Norman P. Tanner, Barbara W. Tuchman, Evelyn Underhill, Benedicta Ward, Siegfried Wenzel, and Herbert Brook Workman, among so many others. Great thanks are also due to my editor at

InterVarsity Press, Dr. David W. McNutt, who first invited me to write *An Explorer's Guide to Julian of Norwich*. His knowledge of Scripture and the Christian mystical tradition, his insightful commentary, and his professional courtesy have enabled every phase of this project to proceed in joyful collaboration. The entire IVP production, design, and marketing team also deserves kudos for their outstanding dedication.

Most of all, I am profoundly grateful for my devoted husband of over forty years, Frederick Rolf, whose faith and unconditional love have empowered every creative work I have ever undertaken. He is my closest confidant and keenest critic. I am also deeply thankful for our son, David Joseph, whose sound advice and delightful humor lift up my heart. What boundless joy David and his wife, Leigh Rawdon, and their children, Adam and Matthew, impart to our lives! Finally, I give heartfelt thanks for our daughter, Eva Natanya, PhD, whose theological insight and spiritual wisdom inspire every aspect of my work and practice of meditation. Such "children are a blessing and a gift from the LORD" (Ps 127:3 CEV).

Part One

Getting to Know
JULIAN OF NORWICH

Why Julian Now?

What is it about Julian that speaks to us today? Why are her fourteenth-century *Revelations of Divine Love* so relevant to us in the twenty-first century? What is Julian telling us that we desperately need to hear in our violent, suffering world? During our exploration of Julian's *Revelations*, I expect we will discover answers to these questions. But first, let me tell you how I heard about this extraordinary woman and how she became a major source of inspiration for me. I sincerely hope that through this book she will become an inspiration for you as well.

Julian has been a presence in my life since high school. I attended a private academy in New York City where I learned to think long and hard about everything and to be unafraid of asking tough questions. My favorite theology teacher used to quote Julian to me whenever I was in crisis: "All shall be well, and all shall be well, and all manner of thing shall be well." Considering that from the time I was nine years old I was a professional actress on Broadway and television, and taking into account that all through high school I was trying to juggle adolescence with acting and academics, you can imagine that I was in crisis a lot! I drew great comfort from Julian's words; yet all that time, I never really knew who Julian was.

Jump cut to the late 1970s. As a young wife and mother, I finally read Julian's *Revelations* and was overwhelmed by her passionate questioning (just like my own), her luminous faith, her buoyant hope, and her large-heartedness. Julian struck me as an immensely courageous woman. Most of all, in every one of Julian's sixteen revelations of Christ on the cross, I heard, for the first time, the gospel in a woman's voice and from a woman's point of view. That was life-changing. I read Julian's Short and Long Texts over and over again, for decades. My children remember seeing the *Revelations* next to the Bible on my reading table the whole time they were growing up. It was the sound of Julian's voice, speaking to me directly off the page, that strengthened and guided me through some very difficult times. Here was a theologian, and (as I became convinced through my research) a wife and mother, who dared to write about God in maternal terms from her own deep experience of being a mother. Julian became my spiritual mentor and my friend.

For years, I taught Julian's *Revelations* in courses on the history of Christian mysticism. Students, both male and female, were deeply struck by Julian's brilliance of mind and warmth of heart, responding very personally to her profound understanding of why and how "all shall be well." I've also led retreats with Julian for groups of all ages and religious affiliations. I've found that both students and retreatants want to know more about Julian's medieval world and what kind of life she might have lived, and to be guided into her sometimes challenging text, precisely so they can relate the *Revelations* more directly to their own spiritual paths. It is this live audience that inspired me to write my first book on Julian: *Julian's Gospel: Illuminating the Life & Revelations of Julian of Norwich.*

While doing exhaustive historical research on every aspect of the fourteenth century that could possibly throw light on Julian's life, I continued to delve into Julian's text and subtext for hidden clues to her mind, her heart, and her story. I wanted to bring this fascinating woman to life by reconstructing a personal history in a dramatic and poignant way that could resonate with modern readers. I also wished to provide contemporary men and women with the necessary theological explanations and spiritual context in order to experience Julian's text on a deeply personal level. After four years of research and writing, *Julian's Gospel* became the first book to combine an in-depth historical reconstruction of Julian's life in fourteenth century Norwich alongside a chapter-by-chapter exegesis of her *Revelations* (using my new translation of Julian's text from the Middle English). Now I offer you a concise but still comprehensive investigation of Julian's *Revelations* in this *Explorer's Guide.*

Julian's "Three Gifts"

Let us begin where Julian begins. In a matter-of-fact tone, she tells us that she was nobody special, "a simple creature that could [read] no letter" (that is, she could not read *Latin*).[1] She writes that the revelations were shown to her in "the year of our Lord 1373, the eighth day of May."[2] However, before she relates her visionary experiences, Julian shares some personal background information with her readers. In the process, she reveals how devout—and daring!—she was as a young girl. She had "earlier desired three gifts of God. The first was the mind of his passion. The second was bodily sickness in youth at thirty years of age. The third was to have of God's gift three wounds": true contrition, natural compassion, and a longing for God.[3] In other words, she wanted to be spiritually wounded by a genuine sorrow for sin, a willingness to perform the

---

[1] Georgia Ronan Crampton, ed., *The Shewings of Julian of Norwich*, ed. Georgia Ronan Crampton, TEAMS Middle English Texts Series (Kalamazoo: Western Michigan University, Medieval Institute Publications, 1994), Sloane Text, II:42.39. All translations of this Middle English text are my own.

[2] Crampton, *Shewings*, II:42-43.39.

[3] Crampton, *Shewings*, II:43-45.39.

corporal and spiritual works of mercy towards her fellow human beings, and an all-consuming desire to love God with all her heart, with all her soul, with all her mind, and with all her strength (Mk 12:30, Lk 10:27, Mt 22:37, Deut 6:5).

Julian explains that she already had some feeling for the passion of Christ, but she wanted to experience more, "by the grace of God." She longed to be like Mary Magdalene and the other women whom she described as "Christ's lovers," standing at the foot of the cross, so that she "could have seen bodily the passion that our lord suffered for me, that I might have suffered with him as others did that loved him" (2:8-10.125-127).[4] This was the first gift she requested:

> And therefore I desired *a bodily sight*, wherein I might have more knowing [greater understanding] of the bodily pains of our savior, and of the compassion of our lady [Christ's mother] and of all his true lovers that were living at that time and saw his pains. For I would have been one of them and have suffered with them. (2:10-13.127, emphasis added)

Surely Julian did not make such a request because she thought she deserved a vision for being devout. She was quick to add that she never asked for another *shewing* (her word for a visionary experience) until she would see God at her death, for she believed firmly she would be saved by God's mercy. She simply wanted to have a physical sight of Christ on the cross in order to share his sufferings more intimately and to love him more deeply. She was convinced that after such a bodily vision she would have a truer understanding of and sympathy for all that the Lord had endured for our sins. This was "the mind of the passion" Julian longed for: to undergo in some

---

[4]See Nicholas Watson and Jacqueline Jenkins, eds., *The Writings of Julian of Norwich: A Vision Showed to a Devout Woman and A Revelation of Love* (University Park: Pennsylvania State University Press, 2006). Except where footnoted, I will reference this critical text throughout *An Explorer's Guide to Julian of Norwich* as the source of my own translations.

measure what Mary Magdalene and the other "true lovers" of Christ saw, heard, and felt at the crucifixion. In other words, like so many of us, she didn't just want theoretical knowledge; she craved real *experience*.

> In the Short Text, Julian called her mystical experiences *shewings*, an older English word that meant "manifestations." These came to her as bodily sights of Christ on the cross; in locutions or words that she heard spoken directly by Christ; and in intellectual and spiritual understandings that continued to develop throughout the rest of her long life. Julian considered all her mystical experiences to be direct *shewings* from God.

The second gift presents more of a problem: Julian requested "a bodily sickness" from God. She didn't desire merely a token illness, but one that would be "near death," so that she would receive the last rites, fully expecting to die, surrounded by her loved ones also convinced she would die. She wanted all kinds of the pain, both physical and spiritual, that she and most Christians of her time were taught to expect at death; that is, terrors and temptations by devils and every other possible kind of agony "except the outpassing of the soul"; that is, except the actual separation of the soul from the body in death (2:24.127). Julian certainly had a vivid imagination! She longed to suffer through all this so that she might be "purged [of sin] by the mercy of God, and afterward live more to the worshippe of God because of that sickness, for I hoped that it might be a help to me when I should die" (2:25-27.127-129).

Julian insists that this idea came "freely, without any seeking" as a graced inspiration (2:17.127). Nevertheless, she must have been influenced by the ardent devotion to the *imitatio Christi* (imitation of

Christ) that pervaded religious literature throughout the medieval period. St. Bernard of Clairvaux (1090–1153) in his *Sermons on the Song of Songs* encouraged his Cistercian monks to use their imaginations to recreate vivid scenes from the life, death, and resurrection of Jesus Christ in order to increase their love of virtue, expel carnal vices, and combat temptations. St. Francis of Assisi (ca. 1181–1226) focused his own spirituality, and that of his friars, on the imitation of Christ's poverty, humility, love of the marginalized, and most especially on his sorrows and sufferings. St. Bonaventure (1221–1274), who became minister General of the Franciscan Order of Friars Minor, considered that meditating on the passion was essential for anyone who wished to burn with love for Christ.

In Julian's own fourteenth century, meditation manuals proliferated, not only for parish priests and cloistered nuns and monks, but also for the laity. They urged the faithful to enter deeply into the scenes of Christ's passion and death through imagination and recollection. Older Latin *Meditations on the Life of Christ* were translated into English so that they could be preached in vernacular sermons and used as private devotions. Richard Rolle (ca. 1290–1349), the English hermit of Hampole, wrote his own vernacular series of *Meditations on the Passion*, which depicted the sufferings of Christ in particularly gruesome detail. Perhaps the most revered religious manual of the time was *Meditationes Vitae Christi*, sections of which were translated into Middle English rhyming couplets in the early fourteenth century and eventually rendered in English prose around 1400 as *The Mirrour of the Blessed Lyfe of Jesu* by Nicholas Love. All these manuals were designed to arouse in the soul a deep repentance for sin, a profound identification with the sufferings of Christ on the cross, and a burning desire to devote one's life to God. In the fifteenth century, such meditation manuals culminated in *The Imitation of Christ*, a classic work of piety by Thomas à Kempis (1380–1471). As a result of this practice of "affective devotion" every true Christian, like the early martyrs, was supposed to be ready to suffer anything and everything in imitation of Christ—even death.

At first, it might seem to us that Julian internalized this spiritual goal of martyrdom to an inordinate degree, perhaps dangerously so, in accordance with some of the extreme ascetical practices of the time. She might have been led to flagellate herself as did so many medieval mystics. She might have starved herself into a mystical experience, like the *anorexia mirabilis* (marvelous fasting) women who reportedly ate only the Eucharist for sustenance. (St. Catherine of Siena was one of these.) She might have pierced her head with a crown of thorns, driven nails into her flesh, deprived herself of sleep and food, or tried any number of other severe measures to bring on a deathly illness.

Thankfully, we have no evidence that Julian ever advocated or engaged in any extreme penitential practices whatsoever. On the contrary, Julian comes through her writings as the healthiest, most well-balanced woman imaginable. (Maybe that's why she lived well into her seventies, surviving at least five cycles of the bubonic plague.) Julian strongly advocates "overpassing" the inevitable sufferings of this life, not indulging in or intensifying them. She counsels the utmost respect for the holiness of the human body. She teaches that there are many ways besides suffering for its own sake to be a true imitator of Christ. In fact, when writing the Long Text of her *Revelations* decades later, Julian admits that her desires for a bodily vision and a near-death experience were *conditional*. Perhaps, looking back, she realized that in her youth she had been somewhat presumptuous, even rash. (How many of us have asked God for a gift that was rash?)

These two desires of the passion and of the sickness that I desired of him were *with a condition*. For it seemed to me this was

not the common course of prayer. Therefore I said: "Lord, thou
knowest what I would want. If it be thy will that I have it, grant
it to me, And if it be not thy will, good lord, be not displeased,
for I will not but as thou wilt." (2:28-31.129, emphasis added)

Fortunately, Julian prayed in imitation of Christ in the Garden of
Gethsemane: "Yet, not my will but yours be done" (Lk 22:42; Mt
26:39). That saved her from her own early tendency to ascetic extremes. Yet Julian adds explicitly that she had wanted to have this
sickness when she was "thirty years old" (2:31.129). As we shall see,
this youthful desire proved to be prophetic after all. By her own
account, Julian experienced a near-death illness exactly at thirty
and a half years old.

For the third gift, Julian was inspired by a sermon she heard
about St. Cecilia who suffered three wounds to her neck and died
a martyr in the second century. Julian conceived "a mighty desire"
to have three *spiritual*, not physical, wounds:

For the third [gift], by the grace of God and the teaching of
holy church, I conceived a mighty desire to receive three
wounds in my life, that is to say, the wound of true contrition,
the wound of natural compassion, and the wound of willful
longing for God. (2:33-36.129)

Because these spiritual desires were in conformity with what she
knew to be the right attitude of mind and heart, Julian asked con-
fidently for these wounds "without any condition" (1:37.129). She
was sure this third and last request would be perfectly pleasing to
God.[5] And then Julian tells us something astounding: "The two
desires [gifts] said before passed from my mind, and the third [for
three wounds] dwelled continually" (2:37-38.129).

---

[5]For further discussion of the religious context of Julian's prayers, see Grace M. Jantzen,
Julian of Norwich: Mystic and Theologian (Eugene OR: Wipf & Stock, 2005), 53-70.

Julian admits that she forgot about the first two of her youthful desires. She allowed her longing for a vision of Christ's suffering on the cross to pass completely from her mind. She didn't remember her wish to suffer a near-death experience. She only recalled the desire for the three wounds of contrition, compassion, and longing for God. And these informed her whole life.[6]

Julian's Near-Death Experience

Julian writes that at precisely thirty and a half years old, she was dying—not just pretending to die, but *really* dying.

> And when I was thirty years old and a half, God sent me a bodily sickness in which I lay three days and three nights, and on the fourth night I took all my rites of holy church, and thought not to have lived until day. And after this I grew weaker for two days and two nights, and on the third night I often thought to have passed [died]; and so thought those who were with me. (3:1-5.129-131)

She had been suffering from an unknown illness for seven days and nights. According to the practices of medieval medicine, her urine and pulse would have been examined; she would have been bled by a doctor and given a strong mix of herbal remedies by the women attending to her. She would have also received the last rites ("Extreme Unction," as it was then called) from a local priest, made her final confession, been given absolution, and received holy Eucharist.

Julian remembers that during this time she felt "a great loathsomeness to die [hatred of dying]," not because there was anything on earth she wanted to live for, nor because she feared the pains of death, but because she wished she could have lived longer "to have

---

[6]For further analysis of Julian's "Three Gifts," see Veronica Mary Rolf, *Julian's Gospel: Illuminating the Life & Revelations of Julian of Norwich* (Maryknoll, NY: Orbis Books, 2013), 225-41.

loved God better and for a longer time, that I might, by the grace
of that living, have more knowing and loving of God in the bliss of
heaven" (3:5-10.131). She might have experienced St. Paul's own
inner conflict between the "desire . . . to depart and be with Christ,
for that is far better" (Phil 1:23), and the wish "to remain in the flesh"
(Phil 1:24) in order to serve others. Julian considered what she had
already suffered on earth to be miniscule compared to the endless
joys of heaven. She even wondered, "Good lord, may my living no
longer be to thy worshippe?" (3:11-12.131). Nevertheless, she was
convinced she would die and she fully assented to God's will.

Somehow, she hung on through that seventh night until daybreak.
By this time, her breathing was labored, her heart rate accelerated, her
pain excruciating, and she writes that "my body was dead from the
middle downward" (3:14-15.131). The women around her bed moved
Julian into an upright position, with pillows for support, to give "more
freedom of my heart to be at God's will, and think about God while
my life would last" (3:16-17.131). Someone (perhaps her mother, who
Julian tells us stayed at her bedside) sent for the local curate, or parish
priest, to provide prayers and comfort at her passing. He came quickly
with a child acolyte, who carried a standing altar cross with the figure
of Christ on it. The little boy might have placed the portable crucifix
on a trestle table or blanket chest at the foot of Julian's bed because it
would remain there for the duration of her revelations. The priest
prayed over her and told her to set her eyes on the crucifix. Julian had
a mind of her own. She writes that she could not speak and thought
she was doing very well with her eyes fixed upwards toward heaven,
where she trusted she would go. Nevertheless, in obedience (and no
doubt with some difficulty), she managed to lower her gaze and fix
her eyes on the face of the crucifix. "For it seemed to me I might
endure longer by looking forward than upwards" (ii:27-28.67).

After this, Julian's sight began to fail even as it grew ominously
dark in the room all around her, as dark as if it had been the middle

of the night. Yet Julian remembers that around the crucifix there remained a natural light, adding that she never knew how. She felt the presence of fiends who might tempt her to sin even as the rest of her body began to die. Her hands fell down on either side of the bed, and her head grew so weak, it leaned over to one side. Her greatest pain was shortness of breath and the slow, steady draining of life from her body. She was certain she was at the point of death.

> And in this moment, suddenly all my pain was taken away from me and I was completely whole, and especially in the upper part of my body, as ever I was before or after. I marveled at this change, for it seemed to me that it was a private werking of God, and not of nature. (ii:36-39.67)

In this sublime moment, she was completely cured of her deadly illness, as Christ cured the woman who had suffered from a hemorrhage for twelve years (Mt 9:20-22; Mk 5:25-34; Lk 8:43-48). Julian knew this had not happened naturally, but only by God's private *werking*. She marveled at the change, but at the same time, she was still not convinced she would live, nor did she fully *want* to, for her heart was set on being delivered from this world of suffering.

Then she recalled the "second wound" she had asked for in her youth, that is, "the wound of natural compassion":

> And suddenly it came into my mind that I should desire the second wound of our lord's gift and of his grace: that he would fill my body with mind and feeling of his blessed passion, as I had prayed before. For I would that his pains were my pains, with compassion and afterward longing for God. Thus I thought I might, with his grace, have his wounds that I had desired before. (iii:1-6.67)

Even though this "second wound" sounds remarkably like the first gift she had requested, namely, a bodily sight so that she might experience "the mind of his passion," Julian makes it very clear that, at that moment, she did not desire such a bodily sight or any other special *shewing* from God. She only wanted to feel the greatest possible compassion for Christ on the cross in front of her. "With him I desired to suffer, living in my mortal body, as God would give me grace" (iii:8-9.67). In this state of total surrender, suddenly Julian saw the figure of Christ come to life on the crucifix. So her revelations began, which we shall discuss in part two.

Julian the Mystic

By now, you may be wondering: How can I wrap my postmodern mind around the revelations of a medieval mystic? Indeed, it may require quite a leap. But consider this: What if you could travel back to the fourteenth century, enter medieval Norwich, and become immersed in the sights, sounds, smells, tastes, and tactile experiences of Julian's world? Imagine seeing what Julian saw, hearing what she heard, and feeling what she felt during her visions. How might her vivid experiences of Christ on the cross transform your life as they did Julian's?

> In the Long Text, Julian used a fairly new Middle English word for her mystical experiences that came into use in the 1380s: *revelations*. This word implied both visionary and prophetic pronouncements believed to be of divine origin. In Julian's Long Text, *revelations* referred to her book, to the revelations taken as a whole, and to each of the sixteen individual revelations.[7]

We take such imaginative journeys all the time. Through films, plays, television series, and books, we break out of our self-enclosed

---

[7]See Watson and Jenkins, *Writings of Julian of Norwich*, side note on 1:1.122.

world and enter different dimensions that suggest almost-unthinkable possibilities. We venture into the lives of people who at first may seem strange or positively alien to us, only to discover that once we grasp their motivations, feel their inner conflicts, and share some of their deepest longings, we are able to sympathize with them. We may even *identify* with them.

Likewise, if we are willing to use our creative imagination, we might be able to enter into the contemplative dialogue with Christ that Julian describes in her *Revelations*. However, just as world travelers who want to immerse themselves in a foreign culture must be wary of criticizing unfamiliar customs and practices, so we must be willing to suspend any disbelief or skepticism that we may have about "visionaries." We must try to keep an open mind about what Julian believed she saw and heard. Indeed, Julian herself will guide us in this. Her disarming honesty and clarity in describing her experiences help make them believable and easier to accept. Layer by layer, she manages to break down our doubts by her directness and our incredulity by her faith.

Julian may be considered a *cataphatic* mystic, willing to engage both rational analysis and vivid imagination in her contemplative practice, as well as to express affective devotion in verbal prayer. Her mysticism is unlike that of the anonymous author of *The Cloud of Unknowing*, the fourteenth century inheritor of the *apophatic* tradition of Pseudo-Dionysius (sixth century). The *Cloud* author insisted that the earnest meditator must abandon altogether the use of visual imagery and affective devotions in order to rid the mind of mental constructs about God or Jesus Christ. Only in the silence and darkness of *un*knowing could the meditator experience God. Julian, on the contrary, by drawing inspiration from what she saw, heard, felt, and understood through her revelations, bore witness to a highly visual and expressive form of contemplative prayer. For her, Christ was most certainly knowable through love-longing and intimate dialogue, even given our flawed understanding. Julian was certain that Christ is present within the citadel of the soul and enfolds us in his love. However, in addition to her visual contemplations of Christ on the cross, Julian experienced peak moments of divine inspiration in which she saw and understood God in a more abstract knowing: as she writes, "in a point." And oftentimes, like the desert fathers and mothers of ancient Egypt, she was blessed by the Holy Spirit with the gift of a pure "prayer of the heart"; that is, entering into a silent, mystical, loving union with God that is beyond thoughts, images, or words.

Let us trust Julian to reveal herself to us by attending carefully to her distinctive voice. Then, slowly but surely, we may experience some measure of what Julian herself experienced, understand what she understood, even envision in our own imaginations what Julian tells us she saw in her visions. This is the real goal of our *theo*logical journey. We may discover it has more to do with experiencing the presence of God (*theos*) than following strict rules of *logical* reasoning.

Julian the Seeker

In the course of our exploration, we shall recognize that Julian is not only a gifted mystic; she is also an intellectual seeker after truth. During her visions, she dared to ask Christ on the cross the burning questions that had plagued her all her life. She even dared to argue with Christ during her visions. Can you imagine having a vision of Christ on the cross, asking him your most pressing questions, and then *arguing* with the answers? In fact, many of Julian's questions are similar to those that we ourselves ask: *What is sin? What causes our sinfulness? How does God see us in our sinfulness? Is God really "wrathful" toward us when we sin? Do our sufferings have any use? How do mercy and grace work? How does Christ save us? How can "all things be well" if even one soul is damned? Is divine love really unconditional?* Questions like these are perennial and, during a spiritual crisis, they can become very, very personal. The strength of our faith, hope, and even our love may hinge on the answers we choose to make our own. These questions must be asked anew by every generation in order to discover answers that satisfy, answers on which we choose to base our whole lives. Julian can help us toward finding our answers by revealing a theology of God's infinite love and mercy that, if taken to heart, can be life-transforming.

Julian the Theologian

Julian has been called a "mystical theologian" because she received her extraordinary insights about God through direct spiritual revelation, not through systematic, rational investigation. However, throughout her life, Julian examined the import of everything she saw and heard during her visionary *shewings*. In the process, even though she had no opportunity for formal academic training as a scholastic theologian, like Peter Lombard (1100–1160), St. Albert the Great (1200–1280), or St. Thomas Aquinas (1225–1274), she became a *rigorous* theologian. She is always intellectually demanding, but never pedantic or didactic. One can hear Julian's voice speaking directly to the reader as she thinks and argues "out loud" on parchment.

While Julian can be as rational in developing her arguments as any scholastic, she also trusts her intuition to lead her beyond what can be proven logically or fully understood. Sometimes she admits she is at a loss for words: "No tongue may tell, or heart fully think the pains that our saviour suffered for us" (20:5.191). At times, she may have felt like the apostle Paul, who dared not describe his own experience of being caught up into paradise where he "heard things that are not to be told, that no mortal is permitted to repeat" (2 Cor 12:4). At other times, Julian seems to circle round and round a theme in order to "chew" on it and savor its taste. This is her personal method of "going deeper." Indeed, each time she returns to a favorite topic, she discovers new levels of meaning. She remains open to the Spirit's guidance, even when she does not comprehend it. Notably, she does not seek to provide a systematic theology or a comprehensive guide to the spiritual life. That is not her intention. She simply wants to share the story of her grace-filled *shewings* of Christ on the cross and the understanding she received as to their meaning. Yet from her forty years of contemplation on the rich content of her revelations, she manages to shed new light on all the major teachings of Christianity. She stretches the boundaries of what informed faith implies, resurrection hope promises, and unconditional love demands.

There is no other theologian quite like Julian. While St. Hildegard of Bingen (1098–1179) recorded apocalyptic visions that tended toward an authoritarian view of divinity, Julian disclosed a very human and accessible Christ on the cross, full of unconditional love and tender mercy. While Meister Eckhart (1260–1328), in his intellectually challenging sermons, sought to deconstruct all assumptions concerning the qualities attributed to God, Julian affirmed that we may readily experience the goodness of God in every aspect of creation, even a tiny hazelnut. While theologians like St. Thomas Aquinas and masters of the spiritual life such as Walter Hilton (ca. 1340–1396), author of *The Scale of Perfection*, left us no writings about their own spiritual journeys, Julian revealed her most personal conflicts and failings as well as her deepest longings. Throughout Julian's work, we discover a daring— and yet most accessible—theologian who questions, searches, and struggles for answers. However, near the end of her *Revelations*, she was able to affirm unequivocally that God is life, love, and light. Through her own dark night of the soul, Julian became a mystical theologian of divine light.

Julian is also emotionally raw, often tempted by self-doubt and discouragement, yet constantly renewed in hope. She does something extremely dangerous for a layperson living in the fourteenth century: she discloses her conflict between the predominant medieval idea of a judgmental and wrathful God and her direct experience of the unconditional love of Christ on the cross. Although she may not go into detail about her daily life, on every page of her text she entrusts us with her heart. Once you allow yourself to sink into the many layers of her writings, Julian will reveal more and more of herself to you.

Julian's *Evencristens*

As we read and ponder the *Revelations*, we sense that it is for *our* sake that Julian went to the great trouble of recording every detail of her highly sensuous visions. It is for *our* benefit that she struggled to find human words to convey sublime meaning. She wants us to see and hear Christ's outpouring of love on the cross just as she did. "For it is God's will that you take [the revelation] with as great joy and delight as if Jesus had shown it to you" (8:36-37.153). Julian also assures us that she is not "good" simply because she was privileged to receive extraordinary revelations but only if, because of those revelations, she comes to love God better. She is adamant that if we, her readers, love God better because of what she writes, then the revelations might apply more to us than to herself.

In her humility, Julian never addresses the noble and wise, but the *lewed*, the uneducated lay folk like herself: "You who are simple, for ease and comfort. For we are all one in love" (9:3.153). She speaks to her *evencristens* personally and directly. She writes especially to those who assume they are unworthy to receive God's special graces and insists that she is not any better than "the least soul who is in the state of grace" (9:5.153). In fact, Julian is absolutely sure that "there are many who never had a showing nor sight but of the common teaching of holy church who love God better than I" (9:5-7.153-55). In other words, Julian is saying that anyone who seeks to live according to the revelations of the gospels and the common teachings of Christianity has more than enough personal revelation to live a life of great love and service.

The very fact that Julian wrote down the account of her revelations (not once, but several times) is a major accomplishment. As mentioned, Julian was, by her own account, "unlettered," which means she could not read or write Latin. She had almost no schooling. She could not study theology at Oxford or Cambridge because in her world women were not allowed to pursue higher education. She had to convey her mystical theology in Middle English, the language of common folk, not the language of the Catholic Church. She had to figure out how to create a language that would express her theological insights—and how to spell it. There was no such thing as an English dictionary. Yet in spite of her lack of formal education, books, or tutors, Julian writes with such consummate clarity, profound imagery, and rich vocabulary that she has been called "the first woman of English Letters."[8] And, as we shall discuss in the next chapter, she did this despite ecclesiastical edicts issued against any nonordained layperson teaching or writing theology in the vernacular, under pain of excommunication or even death.

Precisely because she had the courage of her convictions, Julian of Norwich became the first woman ever to write a book in the English language, and the first woman to pen a spiritual autobiography in English. Even more, this "unlettered" woman developed a mystical theology that was second to none during the fourteenth century and that continues to break barriers in our own time. Anglican Archbishop Rowan Williams attested that "in terms of what her theology makes possible for Christian perception . . . [Julian] deserves to stand with the greatest theological prophets of the Church's history."[9] Catholic theologian and religious historian Bernard McGinn asserts, "Few late medieval mystics have provided

---

[8]John B. Bury, ed., *The Cambridge Medieval History* (Cambridge: Cambridge University Press, 1932), 7:807.

[9]Rowan Williams, *The Wound of Knowledge: Christian Spirituality from the New Testament to St. John of the Cross* (London: Darton, Longman & Todd, 1979), 143.

as much nourishment for contemporary theological reflection."[10] And Trappist monk Thomas Merton wrote of her:

> Julian is without doubt one of the most wonderful of all Christian voices. She gets greater and greater in my eyes as I grow older and whereas in the old days I used to be crazy about St. John of the Cross, I would not exchange him now for Julian if you gave me the world and the Indies and all the Spanish mystics rolled up in one bundle. I think that Julian of Norwich is with [Cardinal John Henry] Newman the greatest English theologian. She is really that. For she reasons from her experience of the substantial center of the great Christian mystery of Redemption. She gives her experience and her deductions, clearly, separating the two. And the experience is of course nothing merely subjective. It is the objective mystery of Christ as apprehended by her, with the mind and formation of a fourteenth-century English woman.[11]

A Voice for Our Time

Perhaps the best answer to the question "Why Julian now?" is that in our age of uncertainty, inconceivable suffering, and seemingly perpetual violence and war (not unlike fourteenth-century Europe), Julian shows us the way toward contemplative peace. In a time of rampant prejudice and religious persecution, Julian inspires us to non-judgmental acceptance and universal compassion. In a world of deadly diseases and ecological disasters, Julian teaches us how to endure pain in patience and trust that Christ is working to transform every cross into resurrected glory. In a generation of doubt, cynicism, and disbelief, Julian offers a radiant vision of faith and hope—

---

[10]Bernard McGinn, *The Varieties of Vernacular Mysticism (1350–1550)* (New York: Crossroad Publishing, 2012), 412.

[11]Thomas Merton, *Seeds of Destruction* (New York: Farrar, Straus & Giroux, 1964), 275.

not in ourselves, but in the Lord who created us, loves us, and will never, ever abandon us.

Moreover, across six centuries, Julian's voice speaks to us about love. She communicates *personally*, as if she were very much with us here and now. Even more than theological explanations, we all hunger for love. Our hearts yearn for someone we can trust absolutely—divine love that can never fail. Julian reveals this love because, like Mary Magdalene, she *experienced* it firsthand. Julian tells us about her mystical visions of Christ's love on the cross and how that love totally transformed her life. Unlike other medieval mystics (who may appear sometimes too extreme, too ascetic, or too intellectual for our postmodern taste), Julian comes across as a flesh and blood woman, thoroughly sympathetic to our human condition. And in heartfelt terms she expresses her profound awareness of God who became human like us, suffered, died, and was transformed into glory.

Why is Julian so appealing today? I think because she is totally vulnerable and transparently honest, without any guile. She is "homely"; in medieval terms, that means down-to-earth, familiar, and easily accessible. She is keenly aware of her spiritual brokenness and longs to be healed. So do we. She experiences great suffering of body, mind, and soul. So do we. She has moments of doubt. So do we. She seeks answers to age-old questions. So do we. Then, at a critical turning point in her revelations, she is overwhelmed by joy and "gramercy" (great thanks) for the graces she is receiving. We, too, are suddenly granted graces and filled to overflowing with gratitude. Sometimes, we even experience our own divine revelations.

Again and again, Julian reassures each one of us that we are loved by God, *unconditionally*. In her writings, we hear Christ telling us, just as he told Julian: "I love you and you love me, and our love shall never be separated in two" (58:13-14.307). Indeed, Julian's teachings have greatly endeared her to Christians and non-Christians alike.

Everyone can relate to her as a spiritual mentor because we sense that, even though she lived and wrote six hundred years ago, Julian the mystic, the seeker, and the theologian is very much "a woman for all seasons." Julian's voice of prophetic hope, speaking to us from the fourteenth century, is one that we in the twenty-first century desperately need to hear.

- 2 -

Who Was Julian?

In order to plunge into the historical context of Julian's text and to reconstruct her life, I invite you to travel with me back to the fourteenth century. What a tortured century it was! It was the time of the Hundred Years' War with France, which actually lasted even longer (1337–1453). Perhaps you've read about the historic battles of Crecy, Poitiers, and Agincourt. These all happened during Julian's lifetime. She never knew a world without war.

It was the time of the first-ever nationwide English Peasants' Revolt (1381), in which an estimated twenty thousand serfs,[1] armed with picks, axes, poles, scythes, longbows, swords, knives, and flaming torches, marched through the countryside and into the cities, leaving a path of burning and looting, murder and mayhem wherever they went.

It was the time of the forty-year Great Papal Schism, also known as the Great Western Schism (1378–1418), during which two popes claimed the papal throne, one in Rome, one in Avignon, and eventually a third in Pisa. In the ensuing carnage of papal wars, over two hundred thousand Christians died fighting one another: "Kingdom rose against kingdom, province against province, cleric against

---

[1]Barbara W. Tuchman, *A Distant Mirror: The Calamitous Fourteenth Century* (New York: Ballantine Books, 1978), 375.

cleric, doctors against doctors, parents against their sons, and sons against their parents."[2]

Perhaps most shocking of all, it was the time of recurring cycles of the Great Plague, often termed the Great Pestilence, the Great Mortality, or, as it became known in the early nineteenth century, the Black Death. This deadly epidemic first decimated populations in China and Central Asia, India, Persia, Mesopotamia, Syria, Egypt, and Asia Minor, killing about twenty-five million people from 1332 to 1357.[3] Then in October of 1347, the Great Pestilence sailed into Europe aboard a cargo ship from the Black Sea port of Caffa (now Feodosiya) in the Crimea that was bound for Messina, Italy. Thereafter, infected traders and sailors from contaminated ships docking at other Italian ports continued to bring the deadly disease ashore throughout Italy. As the raging epidemic cut a swath through Italy, the Italian writer Boccaccio wrote, "What numbers of both sexes, in the prime and vigour of youth . . . breakfasted in the morning with their living friends, and supped at night with their departed friends in another world."[4] The pestilence swept from the Mediterranean through France into the Swiss Alps, eastward into Hungary, and up the Rhine into Germany. It also spread westward into Spain and eventually crossed the Channel into England. In 1349, another strain of plague descended from Norway and infected the Low Countries. Eventually, Sweden, Denmark, Prussia, Iceland, Greenland, and Russia were also ravaged by the disease. A fourteenth century chronicler, Jean Froissart, wrote that "people died suddenly and at least a third of all the people in the world died

---

[2]Ludolf of Sagan, *Tractatus de Longevo Schismate*, in *Archiv für Österreichische Geschichte*, ed. J. Loserth (Vienna, 1880), 60:345-561. Quoted in Herbert B. Workman, *John Wyclif, A Study of the English Medieval Church* (1926; repr., Hamden, CT: Archon Books, 1966), vol. 2, bk. III, chap. ii, 62-63.

[3]George C. Kohn, ed., *Encyclopedia of Plague and Pestilence: From Ancient Times to the Present* (New York: Infobase Publishing, 2008), 31.

[4]Giovanni Boccaccio, "The Decameron," in *Stories of Boccaccio*, trans. John Payne (London: Bibliophilist Library, 1903), 2-6.

then."[5] Modern demographers have verified that Froissart's estimate was surprisingly accurate.[6] The scope of the devastation was (and still is) inconceivable.

The pre-plague population of Europe has been calculated at about one hundred million. Historians estimate that between twenty-four and twenty-five million Europeans died in the first outbreak alone—one quarter of the overall population.[7] Then, during the plague's repeated visitations up to the year 1400, the consensus is that the plague killed about fifty million people, more than all the wars fought in the fourteenth century. To put this figure in a twentieth century context, there were over sixty million people killed during World War II. That was about three percent of the total world population of 2.3 billion.[8] In the fourteenth century, fifty million deaths represented *half the total population of Europe*. For medieval Christendom, it must have seemed like the end of the world. Or the "wrath of God" unleashed.

Into Julian's World

As we have seen, Julian was thirty and a half years old when she received her "revelation of love" on May 8, 1373. Counting back, we may deduce that she was born in November 1342. She grew up in Norwich, East Anglia, the easternmost city of the realm. Settled by Angles and Saxons, repeatedly invaded by Scandinavians, and finally conquered in 1066 by Norman invaders, the city was protected by the winding River Wensum on the eastern side and by two and a half miles of stone wall on the other sides, three to six feet thick and

---

[5]Jean Froissart, *Chronicles*, trans. and ed. Geoffrey Brereton (London and New York: Penguin Books, 1968), 111.

[6]See Y. Renouard, *Conséquences et intérét démographique de la peste noire de 1348* (1948), referred to in R. S. Bray, *Armies of Pestilence: The Effects of Pandemics on History* (England: Lutterworth Press, 1997), 60.

[7]Tuchman, *A Distant Mirror*, 94.

[8]United States Census Bureau, "World Population: Historical Estimates of World Population," www.census.gov/population/international/data/worldpop/table_history.php.

twelve to twenty-three feet high. These walls contained walkways between watchtowers that held guards posted at the twelve impressive city gates, the only points of access into Norwich. The gates were closed at curfew and opened in the morning, their portcullises lowered in times of danger or war. The guards stationed at these gates determined who should enter the city and who should not, regulating all commerce going in or out and collecting taxes on all goods and livestock brought in for sale at the marketplace. In many ways, Julian lived an "enclosed" life from the moment of her birth.

From various clues in her text, we may be certain that Julian was *not* born into the aristocracy. She reveals no traces of growing up in a manor house or castle, with private tutors and abundant servants, fine foods, expensive clothing, and the privileged pastimes of the wealthy, cut off from the daily life of shopkeepers, artisans, apprentices, farmers, and poor peasants. On the contrary, all Julian's references are to common, ordinary things that a merchant-class working woman would be more likely to notice than an aristocratic noblewoman who never set foot in the kitchen. For example, Julian finds great significance in a tiny hazelnut in the palm of her hand, in the shape and color of the shiny scales on herring, in the ragged *kirtel* or tunic of a peasant farm worker, in raindrops dripping down from the eaves of a thatched roof. When she applies the courtly word *courtesie* to her Lord Jesus Christ, it is clear she has no personal experience of this word as referring to the "code of chivalry," which fostered and condoned sexual games and extramarital lust. Even more pointedly, Julian addresses her writings to her *evencristens*, the common folk, not the aristocracy.

Julian's childhood was probably like that of most other middle class children of her time: playing games like hide-and-seek, hopscotch, and blind man's bluff; chasing hoops with a stick; dressing up and creating imaginary characters; reciting rhymes and singing songs. From textual references that reveal Julian's keen appreciation of colors, textures, and clothing, it seems probable that she was the daughter of a cloth merchant—a prevalent occupation in Norwich, given its premier position as the wool manufacturing and exporting capital of England.

The Plague and Childhood Trauma

Julian was just six years old when the first and most devastating wave of the Great Pestilence arrived in Europe. The pestilence was brought to Melcombe (now Weymouth) in the county of Dorset on the southwestern coast of England by a sailor on a ship from Gascony, just before the feast of St. John the Baptist, on June 24, 1348. From there, the Great Terror swept across England, ravaging towns and villages. It reached London in early November, eventually killing some sixty to seventy thousand of the city's inhabitants. The plague invaded Norwich in the spring of 1349, peaked from May to July, and finally slowed its dance of death by autumn.[9]

At that time, Norwich was a vibrant, bustling commercial hub, the second largest city in the realm next to London, with a population of about thirteen thousand. It is estimated that seven thousand people—over half the population of Norwich—died in that first outbreak.[10] Indeed, the metropolis was so devastated by death that it would not regain its population until the end of the sixteenth century and would never again enjoy the prestige of being the second largest and most prosperous city in England.[11] Within the space of just two years (1348–1350), the plague would kill between twenty-five and thirty-five percent of the English population of an estimated six million.[12] The death toll could have reached two million people.

---

[9]Augustus Jessopp, *The Coming of the Friars and Other Historic Essays, Including "The Black Death in East Anglia"* (London: T. Fisher Unwin, 1894), 200-201, quoted in Philip Ziegler, *The Black Death* (New York: Harper Perennial, 2009), 167.

[10]Ziegler, *Black Death*, 170-71.

[11]Ibid., 170.

[12]Bray, *Armies of Pestilence*, 60.

The Great Pestilence was caused by a bacillus (*Pasteurella pestis*), only discovered in the nineteenth century and renamed *Yersinia pestis* in 1967. It attacked in three forms: bubonic, pneumonic, and septicemic, each more deadly than the other.[13] The bubonic type, carried by rat fleas nesting in households, on farm animals, and on ships, was the most common form. It produced high fevers (101–105° F), severe headaches, joint pain, nausea, vomiting, and unsightly swellings called *buboes* in the lymph glands of the neck, armpit, or groin. These grew into large protuberances like boils that became black from internal hemorrhaging and drained pus and blood. Death occurred usually within a week in 30 to 75 percent of cases. The second type, the pneumonic plague, which attacked the lungs, was even more horrible. It produced burning fevers and extreme sweats, constant coughing and spitting up of blood, and it killed 90 to 95 percent of its victims within three days. The third type, the septicemic plague, was less common but the most deadly of all. Once the bacteria entered the bloodstream, causing very high fevers and purple contusions all over the body, the mortality rate was nearly 100 percent.

The sudden onset of the disease and the lightning speed of death struck terror into people's hearts. Death came so unexpectedly and so repeatedly that there was no time to provide proper burials. Bodies were piled on top of each other in graveyards or left outside infected houses to be picked up by death carts and thrown into narrow ditches, or dumped into the River Wensum, which ran through Norwich, with no time for loving farewells or religious formalities. Mass burial pits had to be dug outside the city, giving no information at all about who was buried there. In a futile effort to slow the spread of disease, infected families were strictly quarantined

---

[13]For further discussion of the plague and its toll, see "The Great Pestilence," in Veronica Mary Rolf, *Julian's Gospel: Illuminating the Life & Revelations of Julian of Norwich* (Maryknoll, NY: Orbis Books, 2013), 67-84.

and red crosses painted on their doors to warn others to stay away. If just one person became ill and died, everyone in the family was considered infected. Every day was a possible death sentence.

The mental and emotional trauma visited on family members, parishes, businesses, and monasteries in a walled-in city like Norwich cannot be imagined. With no treatment or cure, doctors were at a loss to help and many caught the disease themselves, perishing along with their patients. Monks living in close proximity in crowded monasteries were especially vulnerable. It is estimated that nearly half the monks in the twelve largest monasteries in England perished. In the Friary de Domina (Friary of Our Lady), near St. Julian's churchyard, not one monk survived. Likewise, priests attending the faithful and administering the last rites of the church were themselves stricken. In East Anglia alone, almost half of registered parish priests succumbed to the disease.[14] No one, however isolated in a bishop's manor house, was immune. The Archbishop of Canterbury and his two successors all died within the same year.

The sudden loss of priests meant there was no comfort for the dying in their hour of greatest need, and no chance of being "shriven" (that is, absolved) from their sins. Many feared the eternal damnation of their souls, an issue that would haunt Julian all her life. Indeed, the lack of priests became so critical that the bishop of Bath and Wells, Ralph of Shrewsbury, wrote that if the services of a priest could not be secured, then the dying "should make confession to each other, as is permitted in the teaching of the Apostles, whether to a layman, or, if no man is present, then *even to a woman*."[15] The church was at a loss to care for its flock. Eventually, Pope Clement VI (1291-1352) granted a general remission of sins to all who died of the dreaded disease.

---

[14]Ziegler, *Black Death*, 228.
[15]Letter of Ralph of Shrewsbury, Bishop of Bath and Wells, quoted in Ziegler, *Black Death*, 124-25, emphasis added.

Somehow, little Julian survived the Great Pestilence. For children in the six- to ten-year-old range, the mortality rate was comparatively low at seven percent. Adults like her mother in the prime of life (early twenties to mid-thirties) also had a significantly reduced rate of mortality compared to those in their fifties and sixties.[16] We know that Julian's mother survived because Julian mentions that her mother stood at her bedside during Julian's near-death illness twenty-four years later. However, Julian probably lost a third to one-half of her family when she was a child: brothers, sisters, aunts, uncles, cousins, perhaps even her father. For all the survivors, especially an impressionable six-year-old like Julian, the memories of gruesome sights and sounds never faded, and the pain of losing so many loved ones in such a short space of time never abated.

We may only imagine the traumatic effect on a small child. Julian must have wondered why God had allowed this terrible scourge to be visited on her family. She may have suffered her whole life from survivor's guilt, often asking herself, "Why did *they* die, and not I?" It is clear from her text that she agonized over all those who had fallen away from the church or committed evil deeds during their lifetime who died suddenly without being able to confess their sins and receive absolution. Were they damned for all eternity? As we shall see, during her revelations Julian begged Christ on the cross to reveal to her "how God beholds us in our sin."

Early Education

As traumatic as the devastation was to every household, once the plague abated, normal life had to be resumed for the sake of sheer survival. Julian had to go to school. In her *Revelations*, Julian refers to learning her ABCs and that's about all. In medieval times, little girls were permitted to sit on hard benches next to little boys, learn

---

[16]Ziegler, *Black Death*, 163.

their letters and write words on chalkboards, sing hymns, memorize a basic catechism, and recite the Credo, Pater Noster, and Ave Maria aloud in Latin. However, unlike boys, who were trained in cathedral schools to learn and sing Latin in the choir and progressed to the study of the *trivium* (Latin grammar, logic, and rhetoric), then moved on to study theology, philosophy, law, or medicine at either Oxford or Cambridge, girls were only allowed in school until they approached puberty. Thereafter, girls—as young as ten—were forbidden to be in close proximity to boys. They had to stay at home and learn the "womanly" arts of carding, spinning, dying, and weaving wool; doing household chores; shopping in the marketplace; preparing meals; and caring for younger siblings.

This is not to say that vernacular literacy was overlooked for girls. On the contrary, it would have been much prized by an English merchant family, both to enable unmarried daughters to work in the family business and as a sign of upward mobility. Julian would have had access to books, but only in English, not Latin (the language of the church and scholarship) or French (the language of the aristocracy). Indeed, for the daughter of a wool merchant, reading and writing skills would render her more likely to make a good marriage.

Even though Julian learned to read and write Middle English, she still could not understand the words of the Latin Mass, read the Latin Bible, or delve into theological books. Nevertheless, from a young age, she would have followed the priest at the altar through the devotional prayers and rhyming commentary of the *Lay Folks' Mass Book*, written in the vernacular. She would also have used the *Prymer, or Lay Folks' Prayer Book*, from which she could recite the Hours of the Blessed Virgin Mary, the litany of the saints, the office for the dead, and evening Vespers. From books such as these, Julian would have learned what happens at the Eucharistic consecration, how to recite the psalms in times of joy and sorrow, and how to pray to God on a daily basis.

Marriage and Motherhood

During the Middle Ages, women had very few rights and fewer options. Even though a woman, like a man, reached legal adulthood at eighteen, a *married* woman was under the guardianship of her husband forever, as if a perennial minor. Without her husband's express permission, a wife could not take out a loan, draw up a contract, go to court, or sell, pawn, or trade inherited or personal items. No woman was allowed to attend a university to become a doctor, lawyer, or theologian. Women were not permitted to belong to men's craft guilds, but they became a vital force in helping their husbands in the trades. Indeed, women were employed in a great variety of arts and crafts, including spinning, weaving, tailoring, lace making, embroidery, and the sewing of church vestments. They also made leather goods, jewelry, wax candles, pottery, and parchment paper. Some women worked as scribes, moneychangers, apothecaries, and even barber surgeons.[17] A widow was allowed by the guilds to carry on her husband's business after his death if she had the prerequisite skills. Many a medieval woman managed importing and exporting wool and textile firms, as well as a wide variety of trade booths in the marketplace. Yet regardless of the major contributions they made to the mercantile arts and crafts, women were considered basically inferior to men by both church and state.[18] Wives were not permitted to open their mouths in church except to say communal prayers and sing hymns along with the entire congregation, nor were they allowed to write about spiritual matters, preach publicly, or teach religion to anyone except their own offspring. Like children, women were considered fit only to be "seen and not heard."

---

[17] For further discussion of medieval craft guilds, see Rolf, *Julian's Gospel,* 55-56, 86, 88, 138.

[18] E.g., Eve was fashioned from the rib of Adam (Gen 2:22), and she was often deemed responsible for the fall (Gen 3:6).

For Julian, as for most medieval women, the expected course of life was to marry early (at fifteen or sixteen), have as many children as possible, and hope to live until the age of forty. From poll and hearth taxes of the period we learn that the death rate for women between twenty and forty was greater than that of men, even considering the high war casualties.[19] This was because pregnancy and childbirth presented grave dangers. Even after delivery, women were prone to postpartum complications and infections while nursing their babies—for two years. In addition, the high infant and child mortality rate was devastating to parents. Among English nobility (with the best medical care available), between 1330 and 1479, thirty-six percent of boys and twenty-nine percent of girls died before their fifth birthday.[20]

The Mortality of Children

By the time the second cycle of the plague returned—in 1361, when Julian was nineteen—she may well have been married with a young child, like most women in her time. Oxford medieval scholar Benedicta Ward confirms that in the fourteenth century, thirty was considered "middle age" for women, "by which time a woman should have been married for at least fifteen years."[21] Ward supposes Julian to "have borne *at least one child*, as married women should."[22] Referencing Julian's description of "a mother's service"—from bodily birth to being always available to love, nurture, guide, discipline, and protect her child—Ward considers that if Julian was indeed a mother, "all the language of motherhood takes on a new and more

---

[19]Tuchman, *Distant Mirror*, 216.

[20]T. H. Hollingsworth, "A Demographic Study of the British Ducal Families," *Population Studies* 11, no. 1 (1957): 4-26. See also Ralph A. Houlbrooke, *The English Family 1450–1700* (London: Longman, 1984), 129.

[21]Kenneth Leech and Benedicta Ward, *Julian Reconsidered* (Fairacres, Oxford: SLG Press, 2001), 23.

[22]Ibid., 24, emphasis added.

natural meaning."[23] Philosopher and theologian Grace M. Jantzen concurs: "Possibly she was a widow, whose husband and children had perished in the Black Death: certainly her tender discussion of motherhood points to some first-hand acquaintance with it."[24] Indeed, the intimacy with which Julian writes about the love and responsibilities of motherhood seems to arise from *personal experience*, not mere observation.

Another Julian scholar, Fr. John-Julian, founder of the Episcopal Order of Julian of Norwich in the United States, has studied, researched, and reflected on Julian for over twenty-five years. He posits that the author of the *Revelations* was Lady Julian Erpingham, elder sister of the famous Norfolk knight Sir Thomas Erpingham, who fought alongside King Henry V at the Battle of Agincourt. John-Julian's sources show that this Lady Julian Erpingham married Roger Hauteyn and was widowed in 1373 (the year of "our" Julian's revelations), then married again to Sir John Phelip of Dennington, Suffolk, and bore him *three* children: Rose, William, and John II. According to John-Julian, after Lady Julian Erpingham was widowed the second time, she fostered out her youngest child and entered the anchorage.[25] Whether or not we agree that "our" Julian was a twice-married aristocrat with three children is beside the point here. The telling fact is that John-Julian adds, "Several commentators have suggested that if Julian herself had been a mother, many of her comments on the motherhood of Christ and God make more poignant sense in that she would have experienced motherhood firsthand."[26]

Professor Ward, who supports my own contention that Julian was *not* an aristocrat, considers it probable that Julian had at least one

---

[23]Ibid.

[24]Grace M. Jantzen, *Julian of Norwich: Mystic and Theologian* (Eugene, OR: Wipf & Stock, 2000), 25.

[25]John-Julian, *The Complete Julian of Norwich* (Brewster, MA: Paraclete Press, 2009), 23-27.

[26]Ibid., 26.

child who perished: "Can one go further and suggest that a child loved and watched and guarded in this way had died, perhaps in the recurrent onslaughts of plague?"[27] Through personal correspondence as well as in her lectures, Ward confirms my conviction that "the imagery of one passage which occurs soon after [Julian's] use of the image of motherhood at least suggests a memory of such a thing."[28]

> And in this time I saw a body lying on earth, which body appeared heavy and fearful and without shape and form, as if it were a bog of stinking mire. And suddenly out of this body sprang a full fair creature, a little child, perfectly shaped and formed, swift and lively and whiter than the lily, which sharply glided up into heaven. The bog of the body betokens great wretchedness of our deadly flesh, and the littleness of the child betokens the cleanness and the purity of our soul. (64:24-30.325)

Tragically, this second outbreak of plague in 1361 came to be called the "Mortality of Children" because of the high death rate among children, and, inexplicably, also among men. Ward, like Jantzen and John-Julian, suggests that Julian's young husband might also have died—"either of plague or in war."[29] This seems highly plausible, since Julian's husband is never mentioned as being by her bedside during her near-death illness at the age of thirty. Julian may already have been a widow.

Between the possible loss of a husband and child, the devastating outbreaks of cattle disease that decimated the herds, the severe droughts that resulted in massive food shortages, and the coastal attacks from French ships and saboteurs, there was no such thing in Julian's life as being *seker*—Julian's favorite word, meaning *secure*.

---

[27]Leech and Ward, *Julian Reconsidered*, 24.
[28]Ibid.
[29]Ibid., 25.

That Julian uses this word again and again is a key into her character. It tells us what she wanted most: to feel safe and protected. It seems inevitable that the tragedies Julian experienced from the time she was six years old gave rise to her deep-seated fears about the wrath of God and the threat of damnation and her burning questions about the causes of sin and suffering so poignantly expressed in her text. Over the years these terrors and questions wore down her body and soul. She could have no rest until God gave her reassurance and answers.

Piety and Preaching

Though torn apart by suffering and strife, Julian's medieval England was a faith-filled land. In the midst of wars, plagues, power struggles, rebellions, famines, and other disasters, Christians prayed fervently for help, healing, and salvation. People deeply believed that God cared for them and would come to their aid. They attended Sunday Mass on a regular basis—in good times and bad—prayed the psalms, fasted twice a week and all during Advent and Lent, gave alms to the poor and lepers, and spoke freely of their faith to one another. As mentioned earlier, many practiced "affective devotion," a form of meditation popularized by the Franciscans in which one vividly imagines scenes from the life of Christ, especially his passion and death, in order to identify more deeply with his sufferings. Meditation manuals guided the devout in the method of placing oneself at the foot of the cross to experience more personally the cruel death that Christ endured for our sins. For most Christians, faith was an integral part of daily life.

Indeed, the fourteenth century came to be known as the "Golden Age" of preaching as itinerant Dominican and Franciscan friars moved throughout Europe and England. This was the age of the *sermo modernus*—the "modern sermon." Rebelling against the ancient homiletic style of St. Augustine, wherein the gospel was

preached to the common people in the vulgar tongue and "ex-
pounded bit by bit,"[30] the *sermo modernus* demanded a high level
of intellectual capacity, acute listening skills, and the ability of
both preacher and audience to hold many threads of an argument
together at the same time. Scriptural themes were divided, subdivided, and subdivided again, along with myriad distinctions along
the way. By employing an impressive display of biblical concor-
dances, a steady stream of references to church fathers and scholastic theologians, and ever more subtle nuances of meaning, the
friars performed a tour de force of scriptural exegesis. Inevitably,
numerous critics preferred the ancient and simpler Augustinian
form of sermonizing, and insisted that the complexities of the
sermo modernus only served to shred and obfuscate the sacred text,
rather than illuminate it.[31] Nevertheless, once the friars spread the
sermo modernus all over England, it became the preferred style for
"educated and intelligent listeners."[32]

To hear these sermons—which lasted three hours—folks would
gather after morning Mass and the noonday meal on Sundays, on
feast days, throughout Advent, and daily during Lent. They took
place in the churchyard (in or near the cemetery), on public greens,
on convent lands, or at the village crossroads, where "preaching
crosses" (platforms of wood or stone) raised the friar high over the
crowds so that he could be more easily seen and heard.[33] The nobility sat on hard wooden benches and the common people spread
out on the bare ground, in all kinds of English weather, to drink in
every word. Of course, there were no microphones, so the friars

---

[30]H. Leith Spencer, *English Preaching in the Late Middle Ages* (Oxford: Clarendon Press,
1993), 236.

[31]For more discussion of medieval sermonizing, see "Preaching and Poetry," in Rolf, *Julian's Gospel*, 168-77.

[32]Jacques de Fusignano, quoted in Spencer, *English Preaching*, 240.

[33]G. R. Owst, *Preaching in Medieval England, An Introduction to Sermon Manuscripts
of the Period c. 1350–1450* (New York: Russell & Russell, 1965), 195-96.

had to have strong voices to drown out crying babies, yelping dogs, and arguing adults.

Julian must have heard many of the sermons given at the Norwich preaching cross, known as Le Greneyard, near Norwich Cathedral of the Holy Trinity. By listening attentively, Julian would have memorized sacred texts and learned how to do in-depth exegesis. She would have pondered the scriptural passages long and lovingly so that when she came to write her *Revelations* they were saturated with biblical allusions. She would employ many of the same methods of analysis as the university-trained friars of her time. For example, she repeatedly chose a theme, made three, four, or five divisions in her explanation of that theme, and then proceeded to elaborate each aspect of her theme with care and precision. She also used the *exemplum*, or parable, to make theological points and describe spiritual intuitions. As we shall see, the parable of the lord and the servant, which became central to Julian's theology, only revealed its hidden meaning to Julian once she delved into its many layers according to the medieval hermeneutical practice of the *Quadriga*: from the literal, to the allegorical, to the tropological (moral), to the anagogical (eschatological).

Julian learned how to interpret her revelations and develop her own method of logical discourse in the only way a woman could in those restrictive times, when the Bible and all books of theology, philosophy, logic, and rhetoric were available only in Latin— through a lifelong process of *listening* and *remembering*.[34] To help us gain insight into the prolific memories of lay people in the centuries before laptops and online search engines, we can turn to one medieval layperson who recorded his own remarkable accomplishment: "I learned by heart within that year 40 Sunday gospels . . . and other extracts from sermons and prayers."[35]

[34]See "Julian's Sermon and Literary School," in Rolf, *Julian's Gospel*, 181-83.
[35]G. G. Coulton, *From St. Francis to Dante* (London: David Knutt, 1906), 302.

Julian would also have been influenced by the immensely popular *Corpus Christi* (Body of Christ) mystery and passion plays. Every summer these plays depicted the entire history of salvation, from the creation of the world to the last judgment, in Middle English rhyming verse.[36] Scene after scene from the Bible was sponsored and enacted by members of the local craft guilds in colorful costumes. From dawn to long after dusk, these non-professional male actors performed on small stages set atop pageant wagons that rolled from one playing station to another in major cities of England. It was medieval street theatre at its best and always attracted huge crowds. There may not have been many lay folk in the fourteenth century who could read or write Latin like the better-educated priests; but *everyone* could become involved in the dramatic stories of sacred Scripture performed in the city streets. Piety was in the very air Julian breathed.

John Wyclif and The Lollard Bible

The fourteenth century also produced the first complete English translation of St. Jerome's Latin Vulgate Bible by the brilliant if controversial Oxford don John Wyclif and his academic followers. The Lollard Bible appeared in two versions: an extremely literal and stilted one in 1384 and a more colloquial and more easily memorized one in 1395. It may be noted that this later translation became the preferred English Bible until the Reformation when William Tyndale (1494–1536) produced the first vernacular translation of the Bible working directly from Hebrew and Greek texts. To the Catholic Church, all such unauthorized translations of the Old and New Testaments were anathema, since the hierarchy had always been convinced that a vernacular version would lead uneducated men and women to read inferior and incorrect translations of sacred Scripture.

---

[36]The Middle English term "the mysteries" had a double meaning: religious truths or sacramental rites, and the well-kept secrets of the medieval craft and trade guilds.

Before the printing press, vernacular books were often poorly translated from the Latin and carelessly copied by scribes, thus containing numerous mistakes. If literate laypeople read faulty copies of Scripture and then proceeded to interpret the literal and figurative meanings of the sacred texts on their own, without the guidance of educated priests, the church feared it would lead to grave *mis*interpretations and spawn heretical viewpoints. Furthermore, English churchmen became alarmed by itinerant preachers who called themselves "poor priests" but who were actually uneducated lay people handing out pamphlets containing unauthorized vernacular translations of Scripture. They became known as Lollards.[37] Already, secret "conventicles" of men and women meeting in private homes to read and discuss the new vernacular Bible were springing up all over England. It may be hard for us to believe, but in Julian's time lay people meeting in homes to study the Bible in English without the guidance of an ordained priest posed a grave threat to orthodoxy.

Condemnation

The Lollard threat was about more than the English Bible. In the early 1370s, many of Wyclif's revolutionary ideas held immense appeal for the nobility. His demand for the disendowment of all church properties, while disastrous for the church, would have greatly enlarged the wealth of the state (as it would for Henry VIII in the sixteenth century). Likewise, Wyclif's insistence on not paying taxes to the pope would have increased funding for the English king to wage war with France. At first, the nobility saw

---

[37]The "poor priests" were dubbed Lollards in 1382 by an Irish Cistercian monk, Henry Crump, after Flemish lay preachers who wandered from place to place, mumbling the gospels to one another. In his bull of condemnation, Pope Gregory XI also termed these unauthorized preachers Lollards. Eventually, Wyclif's followers adopted the term "loll" (which in Middle English means to lounge or sprawl) to describe Christ who "lolled between two thieves" as "the most blessed Loller." Margaret Deanesly, *The Lollard Bible* (Cambridge: Cambridge University Press, 1920), 70n1. See also "Condemnation of Lollardy," in Rolf, *Julian's Gospel*, 163-65.

Wyclif as their champion against the wealth and power of the Catholic Church. But during the later 1370s, Wyclif's views grew more and more heretical. In various treatises, written from Oxford, he questioned the legitimacy of the hierarchy, the teaching authority of the magisterium, and all ecumenical councils. His tirades against the pope as an antichrist grew increasingly vitriolic. He lambasted the monastic orders and the secular clergy, denying the validity of the priesthood, the sacraments of Eucharist and penance, and the abiding presence of the Holy Spirit in the church.[38]

After the peasant uprisings of 1381, the English aristocracy became convinced that Wyclif's rhetoric condemning the "unrighteous lords" (of the church), and his insistence on the return of all church lands to the state for the use of the poor, had been instrumental in causing this revolt. Lords and knights who had formerly supported Wyclif's ideas now saw his antiestablishment and democratizing views as an immediate threat to their own vast properties and civil authority. Increasingly, both church and state closed ranks against Wyclif and his followers. The Lollards became associated with a dangerous political as well as religious rebellion.

Soon after the Peasants' Revolt, King Richard II ordered Wyclif's followers to be completely suppressed. Civil authorities were authorized to detain suspected Lollard heretics and turn them over to the religious authorities for questioning. No "poor priest" was allowed to preach in London. The power of church and state was united in its reaction to the threat of heresy and revolution. The Lollard vernacular Bible, as well as those who preached Wyclif's incendiary ideas, were condemned by the English government. Yet the Lollards continued to preach.

In 1401, King Henry IV and Parliament sanctioned the statute *De Haeretico Comburendo* ("Regarding the Burning of Heretics") at

---

[38]For further discussion of these issues, see "The Wyclif Factor," in Rolf, *Julian's Gospel*, 146-50.

the urging of the Archbishop of Canterbury Thomas Arundel. It was directed against Lollard heretics who usurp "the office of preaching," hold secret conventicles, teach new and heretical doctrines both openly and privately, and "make and write books." Those convicted had to abjure such heresy or be handed over to the sheriff, mayor, or bailiff of the secular court who would pronounce their sentence, and "before the people in an high place cause [them] to be burnt, that such punishment may strike fear into the minds of others."[39] Again in 1409, Arundel issued the *Oxford Constitutions* (also known as the *Constitution Against Gospellers*) that prohibited any preaching "either in Latin or in the vulgar tongue" until the priest or monk had been examined, found to be orthodox, and duly licensed. If an unlicensed religious or layperson dared to preach, he could be convicted and "incur *ipso facto* the penalties of heresy and schismacy, expressed in the law."[40]

After the break with Rome under Henry VIII, the new Church of England also became intolerant of unlicensed and non-conformist preaching. John Bunyan (ca. 1628–1688), Puritan preacher and author of *The Pilgrim's Progress,* was imprisoned for twelve years because he would not attend Anglican services, was not ordained as an Anglican priest and therefore certified to preach, and held a private conventicle called the Bedford Meeting. He also refused to give up his preaching.

---

[39]*De Haeretico Comburendo* (1401). Available online at www.ric.edu/faculty/rpotter/ heretico.html. See also Rolf, *Julian's Gospel*, 163-65, 592-93.

[40]*Constitution Against Gospellers*. Available online at www.thereformation.info/ Arcbp%20Thomas%20Arundel.htm.

Julian's Crisis

Can you imagine what such condemnations might have meant for a woman like Julian? It was bad enough that she was an "unlettered" middle class lay*woman* who could neither read nor write Latin and so had transcribed her *Revelations* in "the vulgar tongue." It was even worse that, by writing an account of her mystical experiences in the vernacular for her *evencristens*, she could have been viewed as usurping "the office of preaching" reserved for ordained, or- thodox, and licensed priests. Further, by developing her mystical theology, she could have been denounced for teaching theology like an educated priest. Finally, she might easily have been considered one of those heretical Lollards who "make and write books"! For any one of these infractions, Julian could have been excommuni- cated, imprisoned, or put to death. Eventually, many were. The fact that Julian was willing to risk persecution in order to convey to her *evencristens* what Christ had revealed to her, tells us that here was a woman of great courage and deep conviction.

Early on, Julian defended her right to speak in the first version of her *Revelations* (the Short Text), probably written in the mid-to- late 1370s, even as Wyclif was penning his inflammatory treatises from Oxford:

> But God forbid that you should say or take it so that I am a teacher. For I do not mean it so, nor have I ever meant it so. For I am a woman, unlettered, feeble, and frail. But I know well, this that I say I have received it from the shewing of him who is sovereign teacher. But truthfully, charity stirs me to tell it to you. For I would God were known and mine evencristens helped, as I would be myself, to the greater hating of sin and loving of God. But because I am a woman should I therefore believe that I should not tell you the goodness of God, since I saw in that same time [of the revelations] that it is his will that it be known? (vi:35-42.75)

Yet as confident as Julian was in writing these words in the 1370s, it is remarkable to note that when she wrote her Long Text some twenty years later, in the mid-to-late 1390s (after the second version of the Lollard Bible had been published and condemned), Julian *removed* this outspoken protest from her book. By then, her impassioned and defiant statement could have gotten Julian dragged out of her anchorage and questioned by the authorities. Clearly, she no longer dared defend her right to speak about God as a laywoman lest she be considered a heretic. But still she wrote.

Relevance for Us

At this point in our whirlwind tour of the political, social, and religious tumult in Julian's world, we might do well to pause, take a deep breath, and ask ourselves Julian's rhetorical question: Whether I am a woman or a man, married, in a relationship, or single, clergy or lay, of whatever age, background, profession, or vocation, living in the twenty-first century, *should I not also tell of the goodness of God—*according to my own life experience and personal revelations?

In addition we might consider: If I were maligned, persecuted, or even condemned for speaking and writing what I firmly believe to be the revealed truth of Jesus Christ and his church, am I willing to suffer the consequences? These are not simply theoretical questions. They are important existential questions all of us must ask, especially in our increasingly secular age. What are we willing to risk in order to speak and live according to what we believe? I hope that Julian's *Revelations* will inform our answers to such questions.

Intriguing Questions About Julian

Was Julian her real name?

We cannot be sure about this. Julian may have taken the name of the small medieval Church of St. Julian when she entered the anchorage there. However, it is equally possible that Julian was her baptismal name. In medieval times, male names were frequently given to female children in honor of a family member, patron, or recently deceased relative. The most convincing argument for Julian being her real name comes from the writer of the colophon to the Short Text. The scribe testifies (*during Julian's lifetime*) that the author "is a devout woman, and her name is Julian" (i 63). We have no reason to doubt the scribe.

Was Julian a Benedictine nun?

There is no proof that Julian was ever a nun, either at Carrow Benedictine Priory just outside the walls of Norwich or anywhere else. On the contrary, all the evidence (as we shall see from her text) points to the fact that she was *not* a nun, but a wife and mother. Very few townswomen became nuns in the fourteenth century other than some of the poorer middle class who did menial tasks for the nuns as "lay sisters." The large dowry required to enter a convent meant that most nuns came from the aristocracy or the county gentry. As argued previously, Julian was not of the nobility.

Medieval scholar Benedicta Ward asserts that Julian's texts bear "no mark at all" of having been written in a monastic environment or of having been copied by scribes in a *scriptorium* attached to a nunnery.[1] In her *Revelations*, Julian does not allude to any aspect of the cloistered life or of the delights or difficulties of living a monastic rule, nor does she mention having taken vows of poverty, chastity, or obedience.[2] She never praises the virtues of the celibate life above the married state, nor does she espouse any particular practice of ascetic devotion. She does not speak of seeking permission from a mother abbess to write her *Revelations*, nor does she indicate that she was commanded to record them under obedience (as were St. Teresa of Avila and St. Thérèse of Lisieux). Also, Julian never states her willingness to submit her manuscript to ecclesiastical scrutiny in order to correct any possible errors or unorthodox views. It is clear that Julian was writing not for a small group of cloistered nuns, but for the *lewed*, the lay folk, her *even-cristens*: family members, friends, her women's reading group, fellow parishioners.

In Julian's Short Text, she tells us very clearly that during her near-death illness her mother stood at her bedside: "My mother, who stood among others and beheld me, lifted up her hand before my face to shut my eyes. For she thought I had been dead or else I had died. And this greatly increased my sorrow" (x:26-28.83). If Julian had been dying in a convent cell, her mother and the "others" would not have been permitted to enter the cloister and stand

---

[1]Kenneth Leech and Benedicta Ward, *Julian Reconsidered* (Oxford: SLG Press, 2001), 21. See also Veronica Mary Rolf, *Julian's Gospel: Illuminating the Life & Revelations of Julian of Norwich* (Maryknoll, NY: Orbis Books, 2013), 98-102.

[2]Grace M. Jantzen, *Julian of Norwich: Mystic and Theologian* (Eugene, OR: Wipf & Stock Publishers), 22. See also Bernard McGinn, *The Varieties of Vernacular Mysticism (1350–1550)* (New York: Herder & Herder, 2012), 428.

around her. She would have been surrounded by the mother abbess and her religious sisters.[3] In addition, Julian writes, "They that were with me sent for the parson my curate to be at my ending" (ii:19-20.65). A curate was a secular parish priest, not a regular (monastic) priest attached to Carrow Priory. Why would a convent call a parish priest? And when the curate came, he had "a child with him, and brought a cross" (ii:20-21.65). A child acolyte would not have been allowed in the nuns' cloister. And why would a cross have to be *brought* to a convent? It wouldn't make sense if she were in fact a nun.

We may also consider that in order to express her mystical realizations in theological terms, Julian would have needed exposure to current religious ideas and discussions with well-educated priests and friars. None of this worldly contact would have been possible within a cloister. Monasteries of nuns were much poorer and more understaffed than those of monks. The fewer than a dozen nuns at Carrow worked hard, cooking and cleaning, tending a vegetable garden, embroidering and repairing priests' vestments and altar cloths, and feeding and lodging travelers and important guests—all this in addition to chanting the Little Office of Our Lady four times daily (Matins, Lauds, Vespers, and Compline). They had little time for reading and writing. Carrow Abbey never produced any theological tracts or mystical writings. "The nuns were noted not for their scholarship but for their embroidery."[4]

If Julian had become deathly ill at Carrow, been miraculously cured, experienced visions, received sixteen revelations from the Lord, written them down in a Short Text, and then, twenty years later, asked to become secluded in an anchorage to write her Long Text—wouldn't the nuns have done everything possible

---

[3]Leech and Ward, *Julian Reconsidered*, 23.
[4]Ibid., 26. See also Eileen Power, *Medieval English Nunneries* (Cambridge: Cambridge University Press, 1922), 237-81.

after her death to have the remains of such a holy nun transferred back to the Priory, so that a shrine might be built in her memory, drawing the devout on pilgrimage? In the words of Professor Ward, wouldn't the nuns have "made a fuss to ensure her burial in their grounds and boasted of it; and made sure of having copies made of her *Revelations* and both keeping them securely, and making them available?"[5] Also, wouldn't the Benedictine Order have advanced her cause in Rome so that their own Julian of Norwich might be canonized as a saint? As it was, none of this happened because we have no indication that Carrow Priory took any notice of Julian or her written *Revelations*. Ward verifies that Julian "is not mentioned in any existing records of Carrow Priory or any other nunnery."[6] Julian never became a household name in her own time (unlike Geoffrey Chaucer), and her original texts were either lost or perhaps burned during the dissolution of the monasteries.

One final point: In the record of bequests to Julian dating from 1393/4 to 1416 (the presumed year of her death), Julian is referred to as *Juliane anachorita*, or Julian the anchoress, or Julian the recluse at Norwich. No bequest alludes to her as *dame* or *domina Juliana*, titles usually reserved for nuns (and only on rare occasions, for holy laywomen). In her own lifetime, Julian was simply "an anchorite."

What is an anchorite?

The word *anchorite* is derived from the Late Latin *anachoreta* and from the Greek *anachōrein*, which means "to withdraw" or "to retire." An anchorite is someone who withdraws from the world to live a life of prayer and contemplation. When Julian became enclosed in 1393/4, she was the first anchorite recorded in Norwich since 1313, eighty years prior. To be given permission to become an anchorite, she had to undergo an ecclesiastical examination to

---

[5]Leech and Ward, *Julian Reconsidered*, 21.
[6]Ibid.

determine that she was of sound mind and body, free of debts, able to support herself by income and/or bequests (so she would not become a burden to the church), morally without blemish, and un-assailably orthodox. Ironically, this examination would have been headed by the bellicose Bishop Despenser, who had so brutally murdered rebels during the peasant uprising.

Nevertheless, as the presiding bishop of Norwich, Despenser performed the Rite of Enclosure, which began with a Requiem Mass in the Cathedral of the Holy Trinity (henceforth, Julian would be considered "dead" to the world). Thereafter, the bishop and Julian, followed by priests, acolytes, and a large crowd, processed to the anchorage. Then the bishop administered the last rites to Julian, along with a symbolic sprinkling with ashes, and gave a stern warning that she must remain "enclosed" for the rest of her life under pain of excommunication. After more prayers, the bishop left Julian alone inside and bolted the anchorage door from the outside. (Julian may have been allowed out of her cell by a servant now and then, to walk in the church garden or cemetery, as long as no one saw her.) As Julian would attest in her writings, "this place is prison, this life is penance" (77:33.365). Becoming an anchorite was formal and final.

What is an anchorage?

An anchorage was a small room literally "anchored" or attached to the side of a church. According to the archeological footprint discovered during the rebuilding of St. Julian's Church in 1953, the anchorage was approximately a 9' x 12' room. Like most medieval anchorages, it would have had a dirt floor covered with rushes and herbs. The furnishings would have included a small cot with a straw mattress, a trestle table and stool, a little altar, a kneeler, hooks for clothes, a storage chest, a wash bowl, a candle lantern, and a small brazier for burning wood or coal during the bitter winter months. Most anchorages had three narrow "squint" windows. One opened onto the church interior, so that Julian could attend Mass and receive Eucharist. Another narrow window gave access to the kitchen, where Julian's cook prepared her meals and handed them to her through the opening (along with fresh linens and clothing, candles, quills, ink, parchment, and books) and

Figure 3.1. Exterior view of Julian's anchorage

took away the waste bucket and dirty clothes. The third window opened onto a small parlor, where Julian's *evencristens* could sit and speak to her through a curtain of black cloth whenever they needed advice or spiritual direction. In this way, even though cut off from the world, Julian could listen to people's conflicts and concerns, offer guidance and consolation, take their petitions into prayer, and impact the lives of her fellow Christians on a daily basis.

Do we have any record of someone visiting Julian in the anchorage?

Yes, we do. In 1413, when Julian was seventy-one, a forty-year-old wife and mother named Margery Kempe, from Bishop's Lynn in East Anglia, sought Julian's counsel at the anchorage. Margery had fourteen children. She had been advised by a priest to consult the Norwich "ankres" about whether it would be pleasing to God if she had no more children and convinced her husband to live a celibate life while they went on pilgrimage, visiting sites in England, Italy, Spain, and the Holy Land. Margery claimed that ever since the birth of her last child, she had been receiving visions of our Lord and his mother and felt called to lead a contemplative (however peripatetic) life. Around 1430, Margery dictated to two different scribes her remembrances of the many days spent with Julian in "holy dalliance

[conversation] . . . through com-
muning in the love of our Lord
Jesus Christ."[7] Margery recounts
how she told Julian about her own
revelations and mystical experiences and sought Julian's confirmation that they were authentic.
Margery's brief descriptions of
Julian's advice sound genuine
enough. However, it is most intriguing that Margery never once
mentions *Julian's* visions or revelations. Most likely, Julian kept silent
about them because she did not
want Margery (who was being in-
vestigated by Bishop Despenser as a

Figure 3.2. Romanesque
doorway to Julian's anchorage

suspected Lollard) to discuss the revelations with the bishop or
anyone else, lest Julian be called out of the anchorage for questioning.[8]

What is mysticism?

Mysticism is a long spiritual path and a slow process of growth, not
an instantaneous illumination. To enter on this path, the soul must
undergo a period of purification of mind, heart, and imagination. It
must be cured of bad habits and freed from patterns of sin. As
Julian will tell us, the soul must be "noughted" of all vain attach-
ments to self and the distraction of earthly pleasures in order to
focus on God. "Of this each man and woman needs to have knowing
who desires to live contemplatively, that he desires to nought all

---

[7]Margery Kempe, *The Book of Margery Kempe*, ed. Lynn Staley (Kalamazoo, MI: Medieval
  Institute Publications, 1996), book I, part I, lines 987–89, author's translation.
[8]A fifteenth century copy of *The Book of Marjerie Kempe* was discovered in 1934 and is
  now in the British Library.

things that are made in order to have the love of God that is unmade" (iv.37-38.71). The soul must also endure times of temptation, trial, and suffering, during which God seems absent and unknowable. Julian will write of her depression, desolation, and dryness in prayer. Through perseverance, gradually the soul will experience greater silence and solace, entering into the prayer of quiet, in which it rests peacefully in a dark awareness of God: "But I have calmed and quieted my soul, like a weaned child with its mother; my soul is like the weaned child that is with me" (Ps 131:2). Julian speaks of the lifelong process of seeking and finding: "The seeking with faith, hope and charity pleases our lord, and the finding pleases the soul, and fulfills it with joy" (10:60-62.161). From time to time, the Holy Spirit will break through the darkness and reveal the brilliant light of divine presence; Julian calls these blissful states "the finding." Then the soul feels itself pierced by an arrow of love-longing or consumed by a burning fire that plunges it into ever deeper states of passive contemplation and adoration. This, in turn, may lead to the ecstasy of mystical union with God.

Figure 3.3. St. Julian's Church, Norman Tower, and the rebuilt anchorage

It should be noted that authentic mysticism never contradicts or supersedes Christian doctrine. However, mystical experience may open the mind and heart to a profound depth of perception of divine mystery, expanding previous boundaries of the soul's intimacy with the divine. Unlike hallucinations brought on by drugs or mental illness, divine revelation is understood to be a work of the Holy Spirit. As such, it illuminates the truths of the faith and offers new insights into those teachings for all believers.

Why is Julian called a mystical theologian?

Julian's revelations came to her not through a process of scholastic argumentation and rational deduction but through *direct experience* of the presence of Christ on the cross. This experience was visual, auditory, imaginative, and intuitive. Yet however genuine the divine inspiration may be, mystical experience does not obviate the task of intellectual interpretation. On the contrary, Julian bears witness that for decades after her visionary experiences ended God continued to grace her with insights into the *meaning* of the revelations. Through active analysis and passive contemplation, Julian labored to understand, and then to convey in words, some measure of what she had experienced. In this way, Julian the mystic became Julian the mystical theologian.

Is Julian considered a saint?

Yes, Julian is venerated in the Anglican and Lutheran churches with a feast day on May 8. While not officially canonized, her feast day in the Catholic Church is on May 13.

Is there a shrine to Julian of Norwich?

Yes. The Julian Shrine is in the rebuilt (and enlarged) anchorage on the probable site of the original anchorage next to St. Julian's Church in Norwich. Built by the Anglo Normans after the invasion

Figure 3.4. Julian's anchorage and shrine

of 1066, with a high Norman tower attached, St. Julian's Church was possibly the oldest and certainly the smallest of the sixty parish churches in Norwich during the medieval period. It is generally agreed that the church was named after the third or early fourth century St. Julian, bishop of Le Mans, France. The church survived intact for almost nine hundred years, until it was bombed by the Germans in 1942 and, except for the north wall of the nave, completely destroyed. It was rebuilt and reconsecrated in 1953.

Today, Julian's anchorage in Norwich is a place of pilgrimage, contemplation, and healing for those who come from all over the world to learn more about the *Revelations*. Individuals and groups are welcome for informative talks on Julian, guided meditations, and private prayer. The Julian Centre is next door to St. Julian's Church. It houses the Julian Library and a well-stocked shop that carries a wide selection of books about Julian in addition to gifts and devotional items associated with Julian.[9]

---

[9]For more information, see juliancentre.org.

- 4 -

A Brief History of Julian's Texts

A succinct timeline of the fragile and providential history of Julian's Short and Long Texts

1373: According to the more popular Sloane manuscript, Julian received the revelations on May 8. Alternatively, the Paris Codex gives May 13 as the date, probably due to a scribal miscopying of the Roman numerals viii as xiii, or vice versa.

1370s or 1380s: Julian wrote the Short Text, a vivid, personal account of her sixteen *Shewings*.

1390s–1416: Julian wrote several versions of the Long Text. While retaining eighty percent of the Short Text, Julian greatly expanded her original account of the *Revelations* with theological insights into their meaning, which she received in the following decades and which she considered to be ongoing revelation. Three quarters of the Long Text do not appear in the Short Text.[1]

c. 1450: The only surviving copy of the complete Short Text appeared in a collection of contemplative works by late medieval writers (British Library MS Additional 37790). While not an original manuscript, the colophon states that it was copied from

---

[1]Nicholas Watson and Jacqueline Jenkins, eds., *The Writings of Julian of Norwich: A Vision Showed to a Devout Woman and A Revelation of Love* (University Park: Pennsylvania State University Press, 2006), 40; henceforth W&J.

the original *during Julian's lifetime*, probably by a Carthusian monk in the northeast.[2] It is known as the Amherst Manuscript.

c. 1500: The oldest extant copy of an excerpt from the Long Text was published in an English anthology of late medieval works on the spiritual life (Westminster Cathedral Treasury MS 4).

The Westminster manuscript was transcribed, either from a now-lost original or an earlier copy, into a southeast Midlands dialect.[3] Even though heavily edited, this excerpt is extremely valuable as it predates the dissolution of the English monasteries (1536 and 1541), when more than eight hundred monasteries, friaries, and nunneries were disbanded and burned, along with their vast libraries.

Early 17th century: Two complete manuscripts of the Long Text appeared: the Paris Codex, which is probably the earliest complete version (Bibliothèque Nationale MS Fonds Anglais 40); and the Sloane (S1) copy, now in the British Library (MS Sloane 2499). Notably, the Paris Codex translated Julian's original East Anglian dialect into the more standardized East Midland dialect common in 1420,[4] while the Sloane manuscript seems to have retained Julian's dialect but makes no mention of her name or origin.[5] Both Paris and Sloane were copied by recusant English Benedictine nuns living in exile in Cambrai in northern France or at a newly established daughter house in Paris.

During the same period, excerpts from the Long Text were included in the Upholland Anthology, also probably copied by English

---

[2]W&J, *Writings*, 13. Note that there is no original manuscript of the Short Text, only this one mid-fifteenth century scribal copy.

[3]Georgia Ronan Crampton, ed., *The Shewings of Julian of Norwich*, TEAMS Middle English Texts series (Kalamazoo: Western Michigan University, Medieval Institute Publications, 1994), 21. Note that there is no original manuscript of the complete Long Text dating from the early fifteenth century; only this highly edited scribal copy from ca. 1500.

[4]W&J, *Writings*, 11.

[5]Ibid., 11.

Benedictine nuns in France. This manuscript may possibly predate or be contemporaneous with the Paris Codex. It resided at St. Joseph's College in Lancashire until the college was dissolved in 1999. Unfortunately, the Upholland Anthology has disappeared; it is either in private hands or lost.

1670: Fr. Serenus Cressy, chaplain to the nuns at the Paris house and later royal chaplain at the English court of King Charles II, discovered an older (now lost) manuscript of the Long Text while living in Paris and subsequently published the first printed version of Julian's *Shewings*.

Late 17th–early 18th century: Another copy of the Long Text was made from MS Sloane 2499 (S1) with contemporary spellings and is also in the British Library (MS Sloane 3705). It is termed S2.

1745: An anchoress named Lady Julian was mentioned as the author of an account (the Short Text) of her visions in Francis Blomefield's second volume of his history of Norwich:

> In 1393, Lady Julian was an anchoress here, a strict recluse, and had two servants to attend her in her old age. . . . This woman, in those days, was esteemed one of the greatest holiness. The Rev. Mr. Francis Peck, author of the *Antiquities of Stanford*, had an old vellum MS, 36 quarto pages of which contained an account of the visions, etc. of this woman.[6]

1843: The Cressy Long Text was reprinted by G. H. Parker with some modernizations, although still in Middle English and therefore restricted to scholarly study.

1864: Cressy's Long Text was reprinted again.

---

[6]Francis Blomefield, *The History of the City and County of Norwich, Part II*, vol. 4 of *An Essay Towards a Topographical History of the County of Norfolk* (London: n.p., 1806), chap. 42, no. 22.

1877: Henry Collins published the first modernized version of Sloane 2499 (S1), making Julian more accessible to contemporary readers.

1901: Grace Warrack published her own modernized version of Sloane 2499 (S1) with an insightful introduction.

1902: Cressy's Long Text was reprinted with a preface by the Jesuit priest Fr. George Tyrrell.

Nevertheless, at the turn of the twentieth century, Julian's *Revelations* were still largely unknown to the public.

1910: The Short Text, thought to have been lost, suddenly reappeared at Sotheby's Auction House in London as part of the sale of Lord Amherst's library. It was bought by the British Museum (now the British Library).

1911: Reverend Dundas Harford published the *oldest manuscript* of all—the Short Text—dating from ca. 1450. It included a short colophon by the fifteenth century scribe:

> Here is a vision shown by the goodness of God to a devout woman, and her name is Julian, who is a recluse at Norwich, and yet is on life [still alive], the year of our Lord 1413. In which vision are very many comforting words and greatly stirring to all those who desire to be Christ's lovers. (i.63)

This colophon confirms that when the transcription of the Short Text was made (whether copied from Julian's own handwriting or another copy), Julian of Norwich was known by the scribe to be its undisputed author. She was identified as a woman, a visionary, and as still being very much alive at the age of seventy-one.

1976: Marion Glasscoe published a scholarly edition of the Sloane Long Text (S1).

1978: Frances Beer produced an equally scholarly edition of the Short Text.

Also, Fr. Edmund Colledge, OSA, and James Walsh, SJ, completed the first critical edition of both the Long and Short texts, called *A Book of Showings to the Anchoress Julian of Norwich*, in two volumes, based on the Paris Codex but working from all extant manuscripts.

1994: The TEAMS Middle English Texts Series produced a critical edition of the SI Long Text (MS Sloane 2499), edited by Georgia Ronan Crampton.

2006: Nicholas Watson and Jacqueline Jenkins edited and produced a new synthetic, critical edition of Julian's Short and Long Texts in *The Writings of Julian of Norwich.*

Translations of both the Long and Short texts of Julian's *Revelations* have continued to be published during the past four dec-

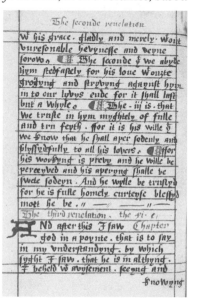

Figure 4.1. Excerpt from Julian's Long Text (c. 1625). Bibliothèque nationale de France.

ades. In addition, there have been numerous theological, critical, and spiritual studies devoted to the *Revelations*. In light of this modern popularity, it is astounding to realize that during and after the Reformation, Julian's Short and Long Texts were almost lost or destroyed. A few remaining copies must have been scurried away to France by recusant Catholics fleeing persecution. Even so, Julian's fourteenth century *Revelations* remained virtually unknown until the early twentieth century.

- 5 -

Glossary of Julian's Terms

Before we delve into Julian's *Revelations* in part two, I want to provide a list of some of her favorite Middle English words for reference. You will see that I have retained these words in my translations, for their vibrant textures and richly nuanced meanings. It's always helpful to know some native terms when visiting a foreign country or reading an unfamiliar text. Consider them as passwords into Julian's language. Say them out loud. Use them in sentences. They will help you hear the sound of Julian's voice.

abidings and diseases *n.* lingerings and distresses, delays and frustrations

avisement *n.* deliberation, contemplative concentration

beclose, becloseth *v.* enclose, embrace, encircle

beheste *n.* urgent prompting or an authoritative order

behovely *adv.* useful, necessary, fitting, possibly advantageous

beseke *v.* beseech, implore

beseking *part.* beseeching, imploring

blisful *adj.* blessed

cann *v.* know how to do something

chere *n.* countenance, facial expression

contrariousness *n.* willfulness, opposition, resistance, perversity

courtesie *n.* politeness, nobility, consideration

dearworthy *adj.* deserving of being loved, cherished

delve and dike *v.* dig and ditch (to build a ditch, moat, or water dyke)

depnesse *n.* deepness of the earth; used allegorically to mean the depths of the soul

disese *n.* discomfort, distress

dome *n.* judgment

domesday *n.* Day of Doom, the Final Judgment Day

drede *n.* fear

evencristens *n.* fellow Christians

exemplum *n.* parable, illustrative story told to convey a deeper meaning

fiende *n.* demon, devil, Satan

garland *n.* a head wreath of flowers, leaves, or thorns worn for decoration, honor, or shame

ghostly *adj., adv.* spiritually, unearthly, mystically

godly will *n.* the soul's essential nature and desire for God that never fully assents to sin

gramercy *interj.* grant mercy; literally, great thanks (from the French, *grand merci*)

grone and mone, groneth and moneth *v.* groan and moan

ground *n.* foundation of the soul, source of being, spiritual depths

happe and aventure *n.* good fortune and bad accident

halse, halseth *v.* embrace

homely *adj.* simple, plain, familiar, intimate, like being at home

irkenes *n.* irritation, annoyance, anger

kepe, kepeth *v.* keep, take care of, preserve, protect

keeper *n.* protector, preserver

kirtel *n.* tunic of a peasant laborer

languring *part.* exhausting, weakening

let, letted *v.* hinder, thwart, prevent, spoil

lewed *adj.* nonclerical, uneducated, unlettered, ignorant, coarse, vulgar

liking *n.* delight, good pleasure

mete *n.* food, dinner

misty *adj.* secret, mysterious

none *n.* ninth hour or 3 p.m.

nought *n.* nothing, zero

nought *v.* deny, discount, strip away

noughting *part.* denying oneself, stripping away non-essentials

one, oned, oneth *v.* bring together two into one, unite

overpass *v.* go far beyond, exceed, transcend

privity *n.* glorious secret hidden in God

rave *v.* hallucinate and hear wild speech, be out of one's mind

rightfullehede *n.* rightfulness, righteousness, justice, perfection

savour *v.* taste, smell, enjoy

scorne *v.* reject, disdain, disregard

sekernesse *n.* security, certainty, safety

seker *adj.* secure, certain, safe, sure, true

sekerly *adv.* securely, safely, certainly, surely, truly

sensuality *n.* psychophysical awareness, sensual powers of the soul

shewing *n.* manifestation or revelation, usually from a divine source

sinne, *n.* serious or mortal sin, opposition to God's will, moral evil

slade *n.* valley, ditch, hollow, or ravine dug to keep sheep and cattle from wandering

slake *v.* assuage, as in slake one's thirst

smitings *pl. n.* deep gashes (from being whipped)

substance *n.* nonmaterial essence, essential nature that makes a thing to be what it is

swinke and swete *v.* work and sweat

travail *n.* hard work, labor (as a woman's labor to give birth); implies exhaustion

unlettered *adj.* unable to read or write Latin

unpossible *adj.* impossible, incapable of being done; or *n.*, an impossibility

unshriven *adj.* unconfessed, not having confessed sins to a priest and received absolution

villein *n.* tenant farmer legally indentured to the lord of the manor, feudal peasant

wallow and writhe, walloweth and writheth *v.* flounder and twist in
   pain

wele and woe *n.* happiness and sorrow, good fortune and regret, pros-
   perity and pain

well apaid *adj.* well pleased, well satisfied

werking *part.* divine activity in the soul

wonning *n.* dwelling place, home

worshippe, wurshippe *n.* honor, good reputation, renown

wrath, wrathfulness *n.* intense anger, moral indignation, as in "the
   wrath of God"

wroth, wrothful *adj.* angry, full of wrath and fury

Part Two

Exploring the
REVELATIONS
OF DIVINE LOVE

- 6 -

A Guided Tour of Julian's *Revelations*

Now let us continue Julian's story. She will describe in great detail what she saw, heard, and felt during sixteen *Revelations* from Christ on the cross. In her Long Text, which will be our primary source, Julian will also include her realizations from at least twenty years of contemplation on her visionary and auditory experiences. In the process, we will see Julian's gradual development of her own mystical theology. Some of Julian's commentaries (and our own reflections on them) will be brief, while some will require more extended consideration.

As you may recall from chapter one, Julian had been suffering from a grave illness for a week when the local curate came to her bedside with a crucifix and bid her look upon it. When Julian obeyed, suddenly all her pain was taken away and she felt completely whole. Even though she knew this was "a private werking of God," she did not expect to live, nor did she really *want* to go on living. "For it seemed to me that I would rather have been delivered from this world, for my heart was willing thereto to die" (ii:41-42.67). At that moment, she remembered her youthful request for "the wound of natural compassion," but she was adamant that she never desired a "bodily sight nor any manner of shewing of God, but only compassion" (iii:6-7.67). She simply wanted to suffer and die with Christ on the cross, "as God would give me grace" (iii:9.67).

▶ ▶ ▶ **FIRST REVELATION** ◀ ◀ ◀

God-in-Trinity

At this moment, Julian received her first vision:

> And in this state of mind, suddenly I saw the red blood trickle down from under the garland, hot and freshly, plentifully and vividly, exactly as it was at that time that the garland of thorns was pressed on his blessed head. (4:1-3.135)

Immediately Julian adds that she truly saw Christ, "both God and man, the same who suffered for me" (4:4-5.135). There was no mistake in her mind that this was a *bodily vision* of Christ on the cross. Nor was there any fear in her heart because "suddenly the trinity filled my heart most full of joy" (4:6.135). In seeing Christ, she experienced the presence of God-in-Trinity:

> For the trinity is God, God is the trinity. The trinity is our maker, the trinity is our keeper, the trinity is our everlasting lover,[1] the trinity is our endless joy and our bliss, by our lord Jesus Christ and in our lord Jesus Christ. And this was shewed in the first sight and in all [the other revelations]. For where Jesus appears the blessed trinity is understood, as to my sight. (4:6-12.135)

In one great theological leap, Julian plunges into the most challenging of Christian doctrines, that of the one God in three divine persons. In this moment of pure jubilation, she recognizes the Trinity as creator, protector, and lover, as "our endless joy and our bliss." Further, she understands that all the activities of the Trinity are accomplished "by" and "in" our Lord, Jesus Christ. She also

---

[1]Julian uses "lover" in the sense of the divine lover, or the mystical "Beloved," who loves unconditionally and forever.

affirms that she was shown these trinitarian activities of creating, protecting, and loving throughout all the subsequent revelations. These are seen as the primary aspects of God's dynamic "indwelling" in Trinity. And wherever Christ appears, the Blessed Trinity—all of *Godness*—is understood.[2]

For Julian, at this moment, theology gets personal. Her life beyond death depends on it. When you're convinced you're dying, theology is not a speculative science. It must be absolutely believable or it is worthless. That's the kind of razor-edge honesty that Julian will bring to all her *Revelations*. Theological truth has to satisfy her, here and now, at the threshold of eternity, or she will continue to ask questions.

How Did It Happen?

There is no way of explaining how Julian's visions happened, and no method of verifying what she saw in convincing psychological or scientific terms. We simply cannot know how the sculpted figure of Christ on the cross took on human features and began to bleed. Julian didn't know herself! All we have is her testimony that in an extraordinary series of mystical but very real experiences, she "saw" the Lord. If we want to enter into Julian's *Revelations*, we must simply take her at her word, trusting her honesty and humility. She has absolutely no reason, nor any inclination, to deceive. Why should she? If it was anathema for her to write theology in the

---

[2]In his colossal work on the Trinity (*De Trinitate*), St. Augustine teaches that there is only *one* God, in three distinct and coequal divine persons. Even though Scripture refers to activities of the persons singly by name, Augustine understands that this is only to make us more aware of the Trinity. Each person's singular activity does not exclude the other persons, since where one divine person acts, the other divine persons are equally present: "because this same three is also one, and there is one substance and godhead of Father and Son and Holy Spirit." St. Augustine, *The Trinity*, trans. Edmund Hill, OP (Hyde Park, NY: New City Press, 1991), 1.3.19, 83. See also "Trinity," in Veronica Mary Rolf, *Julian's Gospel: Illuminating the Life & Revelations of Julian of Norwich* (Maryknoll, NY: Orbis Books, 2013), 268-70.

vernacular, it was imperative that she write the truth. Otherwise, she might suffer and die for a lie.

We may also need to practice a willing suspension of secular disbelief in the possibility of divine intervention in our daily lives. In Julian's time (as in Jesus' time), people believed in the reality of visionary experiences, divine revelations, instantaneous cures, inexplicable miracles. Like the ancient Israelites, they accepted that the Spirit of God was actively at work in their very human lives and history. They did not resent such divine "interference"; in fact, they *prayed* for it. They begged for guidance, for forgiveness, for healing, and fully expected their prayers would be answered. Perhaps this is harder to believe in our age of advanced science and technology. It raises some important questions. Have we lost our sensitivity to the mystical dimension because we don't believe in the possibility of real contact with the divine? Have we forgotten the art of living in a world spiritually "charged" with God? Have we ceased asking Jesus Christ our burning questions the way Julian did because we no longer expect to receive any answers? We may argue and debate brilliantly about who God is in human circles, but do we keep silent and still long enough to listen to the "still, small voice" of the Spirit within?

Julian will help us consider these issues. By the force of her conviction, she will transport us to a more mystical way of thinking, feeling, and experiencing that is not our usual method of perceiving. She will show us that spiritual realities are much more "real" than our "virtual realities." They are grace-filled intimations of our own immortality. At the same time, lest we harbor doubts, Julian will describe everything she sees and hears with an almost surgical precision. She will take the greatest care to distinguish between what she saw as *a bodily sight* (that is, a realistic *physical* manifestation), a *ghostly* sight (a spiritual vision arising spontaneously in her imagination), or in a *more ghostly* sight (a purely intellectual mode of understanding).

Throughout her revelations she will exhibit a keen mental alertness that is a clear indication that she was not dreaming, hallucinating, or fantasizing; nor was she having an out-of-body experience brought on by illness, hunger, or thirst. She will remain completely aware of being in her bed, of the varying levels of light and darkness in the room, of her mother and the women friends around her.

Yet, on another plane of reality, Julian's mind will drop into a vast contemplative space where she is able to maintain single-pointed concentration on the crucifix without any distraction. To those attending to her, she may seem to be in a comatose state. However, she will remain fully focused on what she sees and hears in her interaction with the Lord. For Julian, Christ on the cross will appear more intensely real than anyone or anything else. Her heart will expand and experience an intimacy with her Savior beyond all previous imaginings. And she will become the recipient of sublime *shewings*.

How else—except by divine visitation—could Julian, an uneducated laywoman, have learned the profound truths and been given the spiritual insights she expresses in her writings? How else could she have received direct answers to her lifelong questions? How else could a "lewed creature" have developed a mystical theology that reverberates through the centuries? How else could a middle-class woman have had the immense courage to become enclosed as an anchorite and dedicate her life to writing her *Revelations*, unless they were true?[3] Like Mary Magdalene encountering the risen Jesus on Easter morning, Julian remembered every detail of the Lord she saw and heard and felt. How could she forget? To deny or falsify that transcendent experience would have been to deny or falsify her very life.

---

[3]For further discussion, explore "Seeing and Grace," "Mystic Creativity," "Tests of Authenticity," and "Arguments," in Rolf, *Julian's Gospel*, 260-67. See also Grace M. Jantzen, *Julian of Norwich: Mystic and Theologian* (Eugene, OR: Wipf & Stock, 2005), 76-81.

Christ's Mother, Saint Mary

Returning to Julian's story, at this point Julian still thought she was going to die and that Christ had come to take her home. She feared temptations from *fiendes* but was sure that as long as she saw Christ's "blessed passion," she and "all creatures living that would be saved" would be strengthened "against all the fiendes of hell and against all ghostly enemies" (4:22-23.137). Instead of *fiendes*, however, Julian saw Christ's mother, "our lady Saint Mary"—though not in the flesh as Christ was appearing, but "ghostly, in bodily likeness" (4:25.137); that is, in a vision occurring spontaneously in Julian's *imagination*, yet without any effort on her part to conjure it. Mary was shown as a young girl at prayer, just as she conceived the Savior. Julian glimpsed "the wisdom and truth of her soul" as Mary marveled that God "would be born of her who was a simple creature of his making" (4:27-29.137). Julian realized that Mary was, like herself, uneducated, and without any earthly status. She observed Mary's "reverent beholding" of her Creator. "For this was her marveling: that he that was her maker would be borne of her that was made" (4:3-31.137). Julian understood that it was Mary's recognition of her very "littleness" that made her tell the angel Gabriel, "Lo, me here God's handmaiden" (4.32-33.137). But because the Creator chose her, Mary was more worthy than all the other creatures below her. And above her there was "nothing that is made but the blessed manhood of Christ, as to my sight" (4:35.139).

Homely Loving

Even as Julian continued to observe Christ's bleeding head, she was graced with an intellectual understanding of the Lord's "homely loving." Julian felt the arms of Christ on the cross reaching out to envelop her in love. The Middle English words she uses all imply encircling: "wrappeth . . . windeth . . . halseth . . . becloseth." Julian feels she is being wrapped, wound, embraced, enclosed, and *clothed* in Christ. How reminiscent this is of St. Paul's words: "Clothe your-selves with the Lord Jesus Christ" (Rom 13:14 NIV). However, the irony is that on the crucifix, Christ has been *stripped* of all his clothing and left naked, exposed to the elements. Yet he goes on literally "hanging about us for tender love" on the cross, simply because he cannot bear to leave us alone.

A JULIAN GEM

I saw that he is all things that are good and comfortable to help us. He is our clothing, that for love wraps us and winds us, embraces us and totally encloses us, hanging about us for tender love, that he may never leave us. And so in this sight I saw that he is all things that are good, as to my understanding. (5·7-6.139)

The Hazelnut

Suddenly, a tiny hazelnut appears in the palm of Julian's hand. She has no idea how it got there or what it means. She asks, *What may this be?* The immediate answer is short but comprehensive: "It is all that is made" (5:9-10.139). But how could it be? The hazelnut seems so innocuous, so very ordinary, and thus taken for granted. Besides, it is so small, it could easily disintegrate into "nought," or absolutely nothing.

How could a humble hazelnut be "all that is made"? It dawned on Julian that *everything* that exists is "all that is made": a blade of grass, a cloud, a drop of water, a rock, a tree, a flower, a bird, a fish, an animal, each and every human being. It has taken the creation of the entire universe to make every single thing, including a tiny hazelnut, possible. To make *us* possible. This is the startling real-ization Julian is about to grasp. Still, she is not satisfied. She wants to probe deeper into metaphysical questions: *Why does anything exist at all?* (It doesn't have to.) *How does it come into existence? And what keeps it in existence? What prevents it from falling back into sheer nothingness?*

> And I was answered in my understanding: "It lasteth and ever shall, because God loveth it. And so hath all things being by the love of God." (5:11-13.139)

All physical matter in the microcosm or macrocosm exists—and is sustained in existence—precisely because God loves it. It's as simple and profound as that. Throughout her revelations, Julian will experience this all-pervasive and abiding reality of divine love. For her, "all that is" becomes the *expression* of that love.

The English hazelnut has been around since 7000 BCE, during the Mesolithic Period. In Julian's time, hazelnut trees dotted the English countryside and the fallen nuts were gathered into the baskets. Hazel branches went into the construction of wattle and daub houses, farm fencing, and flexible bows for arrows. Housewives like Julian ground the nuts with a mortar and pestle to make a paste or sauce, pressed them to produce flavorful hazelnut oil, used the casings to measure salt and spices, and followed recipes that called for butter or lard "the size of a hazelnut" in their cooking. Hazelnuts were so ubiquitous (as common as peanuts are to us), *so utterly ordinary*, that Julian couldn't understand why a little hazelnut could have any importance!

Now she considers three properties of the humble hazelnut and links them to her former understanding of the Trinity: "The first is that God made it, the second is that God loves it, the third is that God kepeth it" (5:14-15.139). Of course! There is trinitarian truth to be found in everything. However, Julian does not yet know what meaning this revelation has for her personally, so she asks: "But what is that to me?" (5:15.139). Again, the answer comes internally: "Truly, the maker, the keper, the lover" (5:16.139). Julian discerns that everything in creation is made, protected, and loved by God. Therefore, it is precious in his sight and should be precious in ours.

Noughting and Oneing

At this point, Julian laments that until she becomes "substantially oned" to God she will never know any rest or bliss. She urges us all to be willing to "nought" everything that is made "in order to have the love of God that is unmade" (5:20-21.141). She knows only too well that we seek satisfaction in things as small and innocuous as a hazelnut, where no rest may be found, and "we know not our God, who is almighty, all wise, and all good" (5:23-24.141), in whom is perfect rest. Julian does not imply that we should despise anything created by God, for it is all good. However, we must not make anything our god but God. In medieval mystical literature, *noughting* implied the deliberate letting go of self-absorption, as well as the preoccupation with worldly goods and concerns, in order to reach toward the infinite, the unchangeable, the everlasting good. In modern psychological terms, *noughting* would suggest a willing negation of self-centeredness in order to become focused on the "other"—which is the prerequisite to love. In gospel terms, it means knowing the one thing necessary (see Lk 10:42).

Julian is certain that the Lord is greatly pleased whenever a soul comes to him "nakedly, plainly, and homely" (5:28-29.141); that is, simply, humbly, and intimately, full of eagerness to offer him everything. In fact, the innocence of the child rushing into the open arms of her parent comes to Julian's mind. She pours out one of the most heartfelt prayers in all mystical literature.

JULIAN'S PRAYER

God, of thy goodness, give me thyself. For thou art enough to me, and I may ask nothing that is less that may be full worshippe to thee. And if I ask anything that is less, ever will I be wanting. But only in thee do I have all. (5:31-33.141)

Julian affirms that "the goodness of God is the highest prayer, and it comes down to us, to the lowest party of our need" (6:25-26.143), even as low as our bodily need for digestion and excretion. (Mention of such things is a first in medieval literature.) There is *absolutely nothing* God does not do for us; nor is there anything that God disdains about our body and soul. He knows what we need before we ourselves do. We cannot escape God's love. For we are "clad and enclosed in the goodness of God" (6:37.145).

A JULIAN GEM

For our soul is so preciously loved by him that is highest, that it overpasses the knowing of all creatures: that is to say, there is no creature that is made that may know how much and how sweetly and how tenderly our maker loves us. . . . And therefore we may ask of our [divine] lover, with reverence, all that we will. (6:42-45, 48-49.145)

Christ's Bleeding

Julian tells us that all the time she has been considering Saint Mary's humility and the hazelnut in imaginative visions, the bleeding continued from the crown of thorns in a *bodily* sight: "The great drops of blood fell down from under the garland like pellets, seeming as if it had come out of the veins" (7:10-12.147). With the eye of an artist, Julian records their thick, brownish-red color, how they spread and became bright red and then suddenly vanished when they touched the brows. She compares the drops of blood in their plenteousness to raindrops that fall from the thatched eaves after a major downpour, and in their perfect roundness to pellets and to the scales of herring. Remarkably, Julian is not frightened by the sight of so much bleeding because the Lord appears to her "so homely and so courteous" (7:25-26.147). Like a servant who is treated with respect and intimacy by his noble lord, so Julian feels that Christ who is "highest and mightiest, noblest and worthiest" is stooping down to become "lowest and meekest, homeliest and most courteous" (7:37-38.147-49). And this, in order to bring every one of us up to himself.

A JULIAN GEM

God is all things that are good, as to my sight. And the goodness that all things have, it is God. (8:16-17.151)

At this point, the bodily sight ceased (for a while) and Julian was given some time to contemplate what she had witnessed. She thought of her *evencristens* around her bedside and wished they could see the vision of Christ on the cross so that they might be comforted by Christ's presence. Suddenly, Julian spoke aloud: "Today is doomsday for me" (8:25.151), because she was still convinced she was about to die and wanted all of her friends to take heed that life is short and death comes quickly. Imagine the shock of those around her when the dying woman suddenly cried out!

Julian sums up this first revelation by imploring her readers to forget about her, "the wretch" to whom the revelations were shown, and to take everything she describes with the same comfort and teaching as if it had been shown personally to *us*. Although she considers herself "right nought," she hopes that she stands in oneness with all her *evencristens*.

> And he that generally loves all his evencristens for God, he loves all that is. For in mankind that shall be saved is comprehended all: that is to say, all that is made and the maker of all. For in man is God, and in God is all. And he that loves thus he loves all. (9:11-14.155)

Here Julian makes the stunning affirmation that all who will be saved are one in God and those who love their fellow Christians out of love for God love all that is, since God dwells in every one of us. Julian concludes with a strong confession of faith in the teaching and preaching of holy church. She insists that this faith remained constantly in her sight during the time of all her revelations, and that she never wanted to "receive anything that might be contrary thereto" (9:20-21.157). She may have known the ecclesiastical warning that any revelation would be judged true only if it was not "inclined to any error of holy church, of the faith, or any wonder of new thing."[4] It is even possible that Julian felt compelled (or was strongly advised by her confessor) to state her orthodoxy amidst the turmoil of the Lollard heresies. She is adamant that "with this intent and with this meaning I beheld the shewing with all my diligence" (9:21-22.157). She declares that she received the *shewings* in three different forms: "that is to say, by bodily sight, and by words formed in my understanding, and by

---

[4]Jan van Ruusbroec, *The Chastising of God's Children and the Treatise of the Perfection of the Sons of God*, ed. Joyce Bazire and Eric Colledge (Oxford: Basil Blackwell, 1957), 176. See Nicholas Watson and Jacqueline Jenkins, eds., *The Writings of Julian of Norwich: A Vision Showed to a Devout Woman and A Revelation of Love* (University Park: Pennsylvania State University Press, 2006), sidenote on 9:17-18, 156.

ghostly sight" (9:24-25.157). However, she admits that regarding the ghostly, or spiritual, sight, "I can not nor may not shew it as openly or as fully as I would like" (9:25-26.157). Nevertheless, she trusts the Lord to make her readers able to receive her revelations even more spiritually than she can write about them.

Our Own Revelations

If we examine our lives carefully, we may realize that we have had spiritual experiences of our own, revelations or sudden insights we cannot explain. Some of us have received extraordinary cures. We have been saved in accidents. We have been blessed with great gifts and granted special graces. We have been brought through illnesses, doubts, depressions. People have spoken to us in dreams to encourage us, warn us, forgive us. Perhaps we have also had mystical experiences while looking at a sunset, hearing music, standing on a beach, during Eucharistic liturgy, reading a passage of Scripture, or in contemplative prayer. At such times, we have felt the overpowering presence of divine love; we were given clear directives; we were healed of our spiritual wounds. These close encounters with God bolster our faith and renew us in hope. They become powerful sources of strength in hard times—*that is, if we remember them.*

Unfortunately, we tend not to reflect on our spiritual experiences often enough, so we forget the impact they once made on us. Then even our own revelations cease to be "revelatory" for us. But the soul never forgets anything. Our revelations are always retained within us, waiting to be revived by the work of the Holy Spirit. All the providential happenings in our lives, the transforming encounters, the inexplicable warnings: these are God's personal *shewings* to each one of us. They are precious and full of grace. In order to draw strength from them on a daily basis, we must "go deeper" to plumb their depths—as Julian did with her own revelations throughout her lifetime.

▶ ▶ ▶ SECOND REVELATION ◀ ◀ ◀

Seeking and Beholding

In the second revelation, Julian observes physical details of Christ's scourging and crowning with thorns that had occurred prior to the crucifixion.

> And after this, I saw with bodily sight in the face of the crucifix that hung before me, in which I beheld continually a part of his passion: contempt, spitting, soiling, and buffeting, and many languring pains, more than I can tell, and often changing of color. And one time I saw how half the face, beginning at the ear, was spread over with dried blood till it beclosed the middle of his face. And after that the other half was beclosed in the same way, and thereafter it vanished in this part, even as it came. (10:1-7.157-159)

The clotted blood covers first one side and then the other side of Christ's face. As bodily fluids flow from his body, his skin becomes pale and ashen, his extremities, purplish, then bluish-white. His lips and nails are blackened with dried blood. The impact of the physical reality is impossible to describe. Julian writes that she saw this sight of Christ's passion "bodily, sorrowfully, and obscurely." She desired "more bodily light" so that she could see Christ's disfigured face and body more distinctly (10:8.159). "And I was answered in my reason: If God will show thee more, he shall be thy light. Thou needeth none but him" (10:9-10.159).

This vision inspired Julian to consider that, because of our human blindness and lack of wisdom, we can never see God until God chooses to show himself to us. Then we are stirred by grace to seek him all the more: "And thus I saw him and sought him, and I had him and wanted him. And this is and should be our common werking in this life, as to my sight" (10:14-15.159). We are ever to be seeking (longing for) and seeing (experiencing, finding) God, and then seeking once more. Here Julian seems to be echoing Christ's words: "Ask, and it will be given you; search, and you will find; knock, and the door will be opened for you. For everyone who asks receives, and everyone who searches finds, and for everyone who knocks, the door will be opened" (Mt 7:7-8; Lk 11:9-10). What Julian realizes is that even the human impulse to seek, ask, search, and knock is the gift of God's own goodness. She will return to this insight again when she speaks about prayer.

> For [God] wills that we believe that we see him continually, though we think that it be but little, and in this belief he makes us evermore to gain grace. For he will be seen, and he will be sought, and he will be waited for and he will be trusted. (10:22 24.159)

Julian teaches us that God wants to be seen in *every* circumstance. The more difficult the circumstance, the more crucial it becomes that we seek his presence within it. God wants to be sought so that our hearts remain open and receptive to divine help. God wants to be waited for in patience and in hope. Most of all, God wants to be trusted. Julian understands that the continual seeking of the soul is very pleasing to God, and the "finding of God" fills the soul with incomparable joy.

> For [the soul] may do no more than seek, suffer, and trust. . . . The seeking with faith, hope and charity pleases our lord, and the finding pleases the soul, and fulfills it with joy. (10:58, 60-62.161)

Where Is God in Suffering?

However, you may object: It is one thing to "seek" God in every love, happiness, creative work, achievement, and birth. But how are we supposed to "seek" God in every disappointment, betrayal, illness, tragedy, or death? At such times, the soul feels completely alone and abandoned. Our faith becomes sorely tested. *Where is God in suffering?* Yet Julian is insistent that we must continue to seek God and walk by faith through the longest days and darkest nights. She assures us that even though we may think our faith is "but little" and fragile, nevertheless through the daily practice of believing in God's abiding presence, we will gain great grace to endure the tough times. Julian considers this blind "seeking" of God every bit as necessary as enlightened "seeing." She is certain that, eventually, God will reveal himself and teach the soul how to experience the deep comfort of divine presence in contemplation. This "beholding" is the highest honor and reverence human beings can give to God, and is extremely profitable to all souls, producing the greatest humility and virtue, "with the grace and leading of the holy ghost" (10:67-68.161).

A JULIAN GEM

For a soul that fastens itself only onto God with great trust, either in seeking or in beholding, it is the most worshippe that that soul may do, as to my sight (10:68-70.161).

Julian understands two kinds of divine *werking* from this revelation: seeking and beholding. Both are gifts of God. Seeking is what is given to all of us to do, through the teachings of holy church. Beholding (or mystical contemplation), on the other hand, is given more rarely, directly by God. Julian further defines three ways of seeking. First, we must seek willfully and faithfully, without growing lazy in our efforts. We must seek "gladly and merrily, without unskillful heaviness and vain sorrow" (10:75-76.161), because these are self-indulgent moods that can undermine the spiritual life. Here Julian gives us a subtle indication of her own personal struggles against spiritual lethargy and depression. Second, the true seeker abides in God steadfastly, without "grumbling and striving against him" (10:77.161). This is a wonderfully apt description of the complaints and disobedience that obstruct the flow of grace. The third way of seeking is that "we trust in [God] mightily, with full, seker faith" (10:78-79.163). Julian is certain that these three ways of seeking will bear abundant fruit in beholding. Then God will suddenly reveal his presence when the soul is least expecting it.

> For it is his will that we know that he shall appear suddenly and blissfully to all his lovers. For his werking is private, and he wants to be perceived, and his appearing shall be very sudden. And he wants to be believed, for he is very pleasant, homely, and courteous. Blessed may he be! (10:79-82.163)

What Would It Mean?

What difference would it make in our lives if we really sought Jesus within *all* our experiences? Not just the joyous ones, but the suffering ones, too. Even if people reject us and hurt us, even if events in our lives are painful—what if we chose to trust that the Divine Master is working from deep within the suffering in order to transform it? What if we dared to believe, like Julian, that our fastening onto God with *seker* trust, "whether in seeking or in beholding," gives God the greatest possible worship? Would it not make all the difference in how we deal with our problems? Would it not give meaning to our suffering? And might it not change our mental attitude from that of "victim" to a "loving companion" of Christ on the cross?

▶ ▶ ▶ **THE THIRD REVELATION** ◀ ◀ ◀

God in a Point

Now, in the third revelation, Julian enters a vast contemplative space of divine presence:

> And after this, I saw God in a point—that is to say, in my understanding—by which sight I saw that he is in all things.[5]
> I beheld with avisement, seeing and knowing in that sight that he does all that is done. (11:1-3.163)

In a sudden flash of intellectual insight, she is granted the "beholding" that she had been seeking and receives it with *avisement*. She drops into a "still point" of vibrating energy, blazing out in all directions. It is a glimpse of the ultimate knowing, from which every other form of awareness emerges and out of which all life is created, sustained, and loved. Yet this divine awareness never, ever moves. In a moment of sublime perception, Julian not only *believes* that God exists, she *experiences* that God truly *is* the reality producing "all things." Everything created is a reflection of divine presence, emanating from this single "point," like the hidden depth of a brilliantly cut diamond. No created thing has any independent self-nature; nothing can exist of itself or by itself. Everything in heaven and on earth is utterly dependent on divine reality for its existence and its activities: "he does all that is done." This realization fills Julian with incomparable joy.

What Is Sinne?

Even as Julian marvels at this epiphany, a dark question enters her mind: "What is sinne?" (11:4.163). If everything is created and

---

[5]"This passage may recall the definition of God, originally found in the *Book of the Twenty-Four Philosophers* but widespread in the late Middle Ages, as the circle whose center (point) is everywhere but whose circumference is nowhere." Bernard McGinn, *The Varieties of Vernacular Mysticism (1350-1550)* (New York: Herder & Herder, 2012), 444.

sustained in existence by God, then is sin also caused by God? Her spirit recoils at the thought. Julian quickly affirms that nothing occurs "by happe nor by aventure, but by the foreseeing wisdom of God" (11:5-6.163). It is only because of "our blindness and our lack of foresight" that we *think* we experience good or bad luck. In reality, Julian insists that "all things that are done are well done, for our lord God does all" (11:10-11, 14-15.163). She concludes: "I was seker that he doth no sinne. And here I saw truly that sinne is no deed, for in all this [the revelations], sinne was not shewn" (11:17-18.163).

> *Seker* trust and *seker* faith were essential to Julian's theology. The Middle English word *seker*, distantly related to "sacred," implied all that was noble, true, certain, and therefore, reliably secure. For Julian, the only real *sekernesse* could be found in the unconditional love of God.

However, we may interject: How can sin be "no deed" when it causes so much suffering in our lives? Julian implies what she must have heard preached from the pulpit on many occasions: that sin is a privation, an absence or a corruption of the good that was created by God but that has been overshadowed by evil.[6] Sin does not exist as something created by divine providence; that's why it is "no deed." God is pure goodness; God cannot and did not create sin or evil. *We* create sin and the result of sin, which is suffering. It is human beings who corrupt the good through sinful choices and let loose all the evils and agonies in our world. For Julian, God's *rightfullehede* means that all the works of God are forever *right* and

---

[6]For a discussion of sin as a *privatio boni*, "an absence of the good," according to St. Augustine, see "Sinne Is No Deed," in Rolf, *Julian's Gospel*, 311-13. See also Kerrie Hide, *Gifted Origins to Graced Fulfillment: The Soteriology of Julian of Norwich* (Collegeville, MN: Liturgical Press, 2001), 67-68, 93-98, 166-68.

just. And she is sure that God wants us to take time to behold the righteousness of his works so that we might turn away from the blinded perceptions bound up with sin, and turn instead to the "fair sweet perceptions of our lord God" (11:29.165). Julian sees "most sekerly that [God] never changes his purpose in any manner of thing, nor never shall without end" (11:36-37.165). God only wills our everlasting happiness.

Then Julian hears a magnificent litany that gives voice to the meaning of this revelation. She realizes that it behooves her to assent to the outpouring of words with great reverence, enjoying what the Spirit is telling her, even if she does not yet understand it.

A JULIAN GEM

And all this he shewed full blissfully, meaning thus: "See, I am God. See, I am in all thing. See, I do all thing. See, I never take my hands from my werks, nor never shall without end. See, I lead all thing to the end that I ordained it to, from without beginning, by the same might, wisdom, and love with which I made it. How should any thing be amiss?" (11:42-46.165)

▶ ▶ ▶ THE FOURTH REVELATION ◀ ◀ ◀

Christ's Dearworthy Blood

Suddenly, Julian is plunged from a blissful contemplation of "God in a point" back to the suffering reality of Christ bleeding to death on the cross.

> And after this I saw, beholding the body plenteously bleeding in semblance of the scourging, as thus: the fair skin was broken very deep into the tender flesh, with sharp smitings all about the sweet body. The hot blood ran out so plenteously that there was neither skin nor wound, but as it were all blood. And when it came to where it should have fallen down, there it vanished. Notwithstanding, the bleeding continued awhile till it might be seen with avisement. And this was so plenteous to my sight that it seemed to me, if it had been so in nature and in substance for that time, it should have made the bed all full of blood, and have passed over all about. (12:1-8.167)

She observes that if the torrents of "hot blood" that now covered the Lord's whole body had been flowing physically (rather than in a visionary experience), her bed, and indeed the whole room, would have been drenched in blood. As it was, when the blood reached the edges of Julian's field of vision, it did not fall to the ground, but simply vanished.

Julian considers that just as the Creator spread water over the whole earth to cleanse and soothe, so God wishes us to draw great healing from his precious blood—like a divine liquor—because it is more than sufficient to wash us from all our sins. Julian reminds us that Christ's blood is *human* blood just like ours, and it "blissfully overflows onto us by the virtue of his precious love" (12:14-15.167).

Furthermore, there is *no limit* to the outpouring of Christ's blood. "The dearworthy blood of our lord Jesus Christ, as truly as it is most precious, so truly is it most plenteous" (12:15-16.167). From Christ's suffering body this blood covered the whole earth and descended into hell, releasing those in bondage. Christ's blood ascended into heaven, where (in a mystical sense) Christ is *still* bleeding "praying for us to the father, and is and shall be as long as we need" (12:23.167).

A JULIAN GEM

The precious plenty of his dearworthy blood overflows all the earth, and is ready to wash all creatures of sinne who are of good will, have been, and shall be. (12:19-21.167)

▶ ▶ ▶ THE FIFTH REVELATION ◀ ◀ ◀

The First Locution

For the first time, Julian hears Jesus speak directly to her from the cross in an *interior* locution:

> Then he, without voice and opening of lips, formed in my soul these words: "Herewith is the fiende overcome" (13:3-5.169).

Christ assures Julian that his passion is the means by which the power of evil is forever vanquished. Notice the present tense: while we cannot yet experience it, Christ's triumph *is* already complete—the fiend *is* overcome and (metaphorically speaking) "his might is all locked in God's hand" (13:14.169). Christ's perfect love and self-sacrifice on the cross have already triumphed over sin and death, and rendered Satan impotent. We have been fully ransomed by the *dearworthy* blood of the Lamb.[7] Do we believe it? Are we not still fearful of falling into sin and being condemned by God?

No Wrath in God

Julian's next words tell us how fiercely we must cling to the fact of our salvation:

> *But in God may be no wrath*, as to my sight. For our good lord—endlessly having regard to his own worshippe and to the profit of all them that shalle be saved—with might and right he withstands the demons who out of malice and wickedness busy themselves to counteract and go against God's will. (13:14-18.169, emphasis added)

Julian's conviction that there is "no wrath" in God is a powerful theme that she will develop throughout her text. For Julian, this

---

[7]For more on the medieval understanding of "Sin as Bondage" to Satan and "Christ's Victory," see Rolf, *Julian's Gospel*, 322-25. See also Joan M. Nuth, *Wisdom's Daughter: The Theology of Julian of Norwich* (New York: Crossroad, 1991), 117-35.

revelation was a colossal breakthrough. She had grown up hearing preachers threaten that the wrath of God would send a person to hell for a curse. The Old English word *wrath* connotes intense anger and moral indignation. Wrath was also a biblical metaphor used to express divine hatred of sin.[8] In theological terms, wrathfulness was considered an attribute of God and an expression of divine justice.

However, in recording her visionary experiences, Julian will insist that she never saw the Savior "wrathful." Jesus Christ, the Son of God, did not stretch out his arms to be crucified, suffer excruciating pain, shed his blood, and die an ignoble death because he was angry. On the contrary, the Son of God hung on the cross in obedience to his Father's will in order to effect the ultimate salvation of the whole world. Christ did not die to *punish* us, but to *save* us from ourselves and the powers of evil. Everything he ever did, he did out of love. If we want to know what divine "wrath" looks like, we have only to contemplate the figure of Christ hanging on the cross, as Julian did. It is the true image of God giving everything to save humanity from itself.

Far from accusing us, Julian sees that our good Lord withstands "with might and right" all the demons that could possibly harm or destroy us. He fights *for us* against our frailty, our temptations, our bad habits. Even in our sinfulness, he does not condemn us any more than he condemned the woman taken in adultery (Jn 8:1-11) or Peter after his betrayal (Jn 21:15-17). Instead of wrathfulness, the Lord repeatedly offers mercy. He counsels us gently but firmly: "Go your way, and from now on do not sin again" (Jn 8:11). He urges more daring faith, greater hope, and the loving service of our lives.

Julian knew well that "God is love" (1 Jn 4:8). In her theology, she will carry that truth to its fullest implication: God cannot stop loving us because that's who God is. Unlike the anthropomorphic image of

---

[8]See "Scriptural Allegory," in Rolf, *Julian's Gospel*, 326-27.

a highly volatile God—loving us when we are obedient, then becoming "wroth" and punishing us when we disobey, then relenting and taking pity on us—Julian's understanding of divine love is that it is eternally constant; it does not change. It is we humans who are changeable. We accept or reject or simply ignore God's love. But God never ceases loving and protecting us, even in our misdeeds.

How We View God

The way we view God is really up to us. If we are open and receptive to divine love and willing to share that love with each other, then we will surely recognize God as the wellspring and fulfillment of every love. If, on the other hand, we fail to love God and each other, if we are unjust, unkind, unforgiving, and unfaithful, eventually we become guilt-ridden. Then what do we do? We get angry with ourselves and *project* that anger onto God: "God must be angry with me. God is a wrathful God." What a terrible injustice to God. It may take a long time for us to outgrow our age-old projections of God as changeable, vindictive, and wrathful. Those of us who were terrified as children by the threat of God's punishment may still be struggling to do so. Julian's *Revelations* will help us. In fact, she sees that Christ *scornes* Satan's evil designs on us, utterly deriding their (lack of) power. Christ wants us to do the same. This realization was so liberating for Julian, it made her laugh out loud.

A JULIAN GEM

Also I saw our lord scorne his [Satan's] malice and nought his unmight, and he wills that we do so. For this sight, I laughed mightily, and that made them laugh who were about me, and their laughing was a pleasure to me. (13:19-21.171)

▶ ▶ ▶ **THE SIXTH REVELATION** ◀ ◀ ◀

I Thank Thee

Again, Julian hears Christ speak to her interiorly, in distinct words: "I thank thee for thy service and for thy travail and especially of thy youth" (14:1-2.173). What an astounding moment, that God should be so homely as to *thank* Julian for her service and her travail; that is, her work and sufferings. Imagine being thanked by Christ on the cross for your own youthful love and service, your acts of compassion and generosity, your hard work and dedication. What could be more humbling than to realize that your ability to be a good person and to perform good works flows from the very God who is *thanking* you.

With these words, Julian is lifted up by the Spirit into a vision of heaven, where Christ serves his beloved friends at a solemn feast. Even though Christ reigns royally as host in his own house, "filling it all with joy and mirth" (14:5-6.173), Julian notices that he takes no seat. Instead, in his great courtesy, he is busy "endlessly gladdening and solacing his dearworthy friends" (14:6.173). Julian sees Christ's parable of the wedding banquet (Mt 22:1-4) or the great supper (Lk 14:16-24) playing out in front of her. She is being granted a foretaste of the incomparable joys of Christ's presence at the eternal feast.

Furthermore, Julian is shown "three degrees of bliss that each soul shall have in heaven who has willingly served God in any degree [that is, station in life] on earth" (14:10-11.173) The first degree of bliss is the abundant thanks (such as Julian has just been given) that the soul shall receive from God immediately at death or after purgatory, when it has been liberated from all suffering due to sin. It seemed to Julian that "all the pain and travail that might be suffered by all living persons might not have deserved the honorable thanks that even one person shall have who has willingly served God" (14:14-16.173). The second degree of bliss is that all the blessed creatures in heaven will *see* the Lord's honorable thanking of the Lord's servant, making his or her good works known to all who are in heaven, just as a king might thank his subjects, thus greatly increasing their honor. And the third degree of bliss is the sublime realization that this thanksgiving shall last without end.

A JULIAN GEM

For I saw that, when or at what time that a man or woman is truly turned to God for one day's service to fulfill his endless will, he shall have all these three degrees of bliss. And the more that the loving soul sees this courtesy of God, the readier he is to serve him all the days of his life. (14:23-30.175)

▶ ▶ ▶ **THE SEVENTH REVELATION** ◀ ◀ ◀

Spiritual Oscillations

Now Christ shows Julian "a sovereign ghostly liking" that fills her soul with an "everlasting sekernesse" that was "so glad and so spiritual" that she is in complete peace, ease, and rest—so much so that there was "nothing on earth that could have grieved me" (15:1-4.175).

> This lasted but a while, and I was turned and left to myself in such heaviness and weariness of my life and irkenes with myself, that I could barely have patience to live. There was no comfort nor any ease to my feeling, but faith, hope and charity, and these I had in truth, but very little in feeling. (15:5-8.175)

All of a sudden, Julian is overwhelmed by sadness, weariness, and *irkenes*; that is, total disgust with herself. Instead of bliss, she feels full of despair and impatience with her life. This shock at feeling "abandoned" by God is a familiar one in the spiritual life. Julian did what we also must do in such times; she held on to her faith, hope, and love, without feeling any consolation at all.

> And soon after this, our blessed lord gave me again the comfort and the rest in soul: delight and sekernesse so blissful and so mighty that no dread, nor sorrow, nor any bodily nor ghostly [spiritual] pain that might be suffered could have unsettled me. And then the pain shewed again to my feeling, and then the joy and the delight, and now that one, and now the other, diverse times, I suppose about twenty times. (15:9-13.177)

What a drastic oscillation Julian is experiencing: blissfully *seker* one moment, close to despair the next. Julian writes that in the time of joy, she might have said with St. Paul, "Nothing shall separate me from the love of Christ" (Rom 8:38-39). And in the time of pain, she might have called out with St. Peter: "Lord save me, I perish" (15:16.177). Notably, Julian confuses two gospel passages: Matthew 8:25 ("Lord, save us! We are perishing!"), spoken by all the disciples, not just Peter, to awaken Jesus during the storm at sea; and Matthew 14:30 ("Lord, save me!"), cried by Peter after he had walked to Christ on the water, became terrified, and began to sink. This conflation is a clear indication that when Julian wrote her Long Text, she did not have access to a vernacular Lollard Bible. But it also tells us that she had learned the *sense* of the scriptural passages from hearing them preached many times, and that, both in her joy and her distress, she had recourse to the sacred words.

Mood Swings in Prayer

How often in our life of prayer do we go through a similar experience: feeling the Lord's uplifting presence for a while, then sinking down into the stormy sea of our own predicament? Julian realized that it was beneficial to undergo these spiritual extremes in order to learn that no matter what we feel (or fail to feel) in prayer, God protects us in all our joy and sorrow, for "both are one love" (15:24.177). By allowing us to sense divine presence and then withdrawing, the Spirit teaches us not to crave spiritual consolation above blind faith. Even when we endure physical or emotional pain, Julian counsels that it is not God's will that we fall into "sorrow and mourning for them, but quickly pass over and hold ourselves in the endless delight that is God" (15:27-28.177). Julian understood that sorrow and mourning should *not* be cultivated for their own sake and that a sense of dryness in prayer is *not* a sign of God's displeasure. On the contrary, the Lord wants us to cling to the unchanging reality of his love that keeps us secure, whether in wellbeing or in woe. We are lovingly "beheld" by God, always and everywhere, even when we cannot "behold."

A thirteenth century poem described these oscillations as "the play of love [which is] joy and sorrow, the which two come sundry times one after another, by the presence and absence of him that is our love."[9]

---

[9]Jan van Ruusbroec, *The Chastising of God's Children*, ed. Joyce Bazire and Eric Colledge (London: Basil Blackwell, 1957), line 99.

> ▶ ▶ ▶ **THE EIGHTH REVELATION** ◀ ◀ ◀

Christ's Passion

To enter fully into Julian's *Revelations*, I strongly recommend that you read all of her description of Christ's dying, slowly and meditatively.[10] It is by far the most graphic account of the passion in medieval literature. It is also the most astute observation of the Lord's agonizing pains and the four manners of "drying out" of his entire body that resulted in his excruciating thirst—both his bodily thirst and his spiritual thirst for souls.

> After this, Christ shewed a part of his passion near his dying. I saw the sweet face as it were dry and bloodless with pale dying; and afterward more deadly pale, languring; and then [it] turned more deadly into blue; and afterward more brown blue, as the flesh turned more deeply dead. For his passion shewed to me most explicitly in his blessed face, and especially in his lips, there I saw these four colors—those lips that were before fresh and ruddy, lively and pleasing to my sight. This was a terrible change, to see this deep dying. And also the nose withered together and dried, to my sight, and the sweet body waxed brown and black, all changed and turned out from the fair, fresh, and lively color of himself into dry dying. (16:1-9.179)

Every time I read this passage, I am struck by how scientifically correct Julian's observations were. Even though Julian was not a trained physician, her record of what she saw in the passion of the cross tallies precisely with what modern forensic scientists have

---

[10]See "The Dying," in Rolf, *Julian's Gospel*, 334-56. I also encourage you to read Julian's own expressive Middle English in "The Eighth Revelation," in Watson and Jenkins, *Writings*, 179-93.

discovered.[11] This certainly lends credence to Julian's visual experience. Unless she had witnessed a bodily sight of Christ's suffering, how could she have known and recorded such scientifically accurate details about the effects of crucifixion that wouldn't be documented until the twentieth century?

Here is a brief summary of the physical effects of crucifixion on Jesus' body observed by Julian, though it cannot do justice to her own incomparable description of what she saw bodily in her vision: gradual discoloration of Christ's face and body from the heavy blows of the whipping, which resulted in severe internal bleeding and black contusions; deep, bloody gashes too numerous to mention covering his entire body; blood clotting and flesh falling off from wide, gaping wounds; extreme loss of blood and bodily fluids that resulted in four manners of drying that shriveled his body into a living corpse and caused unquenchable bodily and spiritual thirst. Julian also perceived "the blowing of wind from without that dried him more and pained him with cold more than my heart can think—and other pains. For which pains, I saw that all is too little that I can say, for it may not be told" (17:38-40.183). Julian could only watch: "The shewing of Christ's pains filled me full of pains" (17:41.183).

Even though Julian had endured the death of her loved ones from the Great Pestilence as a child and quite possibly also as a wife and mother, this experience of watching Christ suffer was incomparably worse. It was even worse than her own seven days of painful dying. She humbly admits that she had never imagined what compassion such as this would involve:

I thought: "Is any pain in hell like this?" And I was answered in my reason: "Hell is another pain, for there is despair. But of all pains that lead to salvation, this is the most: to see thy love

---

[11]See "Death by Crucifixion," in Rolf, *Julian's Gospel*, 339-44.

suffer. How might any pain be more than to see him who is all my life, all my bliss, and all my joy suffer?" (17:46-50.183)

Julian is filled with compassion for Saint Mary, who had to watch her only child die: "For Christ and she were so oned in love that the greatness of her love was the cause of the magnitude of her pain" (18:1-3.185). She considers how much all those who loved Christ must have suffered on Good Friday, more even than in their own bodily dying. She also comments that the whole earth with all its creatures, as well as the heavenly firmament, "failed for sorrow in their own way at the time of Christ's dying" (18:14.185). For Julian, the crucifixion was a cosmic event.

All this time, Julian continues to watch intently as Christ grows weaker. She does not know how he can endure the agony one moment longer. Then she understands that his divinity gave strength to his humanity to suffer more than all other men who ever lived might suffer. She keeps looking for the departing of life and fully expects to see Christ's body completely dead.

Transformation

Then, in a stunning instant, Julian experienced Christ's triumph over death:

> But I saw him not so. And just in that same time that it seemed to me, by all appearances, that his life might no longer last, and the shewing of the end must needs be near—suddenly, as I beheld the same cross, *he changed in blissful chere* [his face changed into a joyful expression]. The changing of his blissful chere changed mine, and I was as glad and merry as it was possible to be. Then our Lord brought this merrily to mind: "Where is now any point of thy pain or of thy grief?" And I was completely merry. (21:5-11.191-193, emphasis added)

Julian knew from the gospels that Jesus really died "once for all" (Rom 6:10) and that he could never die again. But in Julian's vision, she saw his suffering visage change *at the very moment of death* into one of blissful joy. Then, when beholding the radiance of Christ's joyful expression, what was the point of her "pain or grief"? The death-to-life transformation was so astounding and so sudden—as St. Paul wrote, "in a moment, in the twinkling of an eye" (1 Cor 15:52)—that Julian's compassion for Christ was instantly turned to ebullient joy, and she became "completely merry"!

That said, Julian reflects that right now, in our pains and our passion, we are still on the cross with Christ, suffering and dying because of our own sinfulness. Yet she assures us that, at the last point, in an instant, Christ will suddenly "change his chere toward us, and we shall be with him in heaven" (21:14-15.193). Then we will not even remember our pain or our grief; it will all be turned to joy. Indeed, Julian reflects that if we could see Christ's glory here and now, no pain on earth could touch us, but all would be perfect bliss. However, until our minds and hearts are transformed through our own passion and death, we cannot perceive his glorified face. Thus Christ must show us the face of his passion.

A JULIAN GEM

And for this little pain that we suffer here, we shall have a high, endless knowing in God, which we might never have without that pain. And the harder our pains have been with him on his cross, the more shall our honor be with him in his kingdom. (21:23-26.193)

▶ ▶ ▶ **THE NINTH REVELATION** ◀ ◀ ◀

Are You Well-Satisfied?

Again, Julian heard the Lord speaking to her from the cross, this time with a question:

> Then said our good lord, asking: "Art thou well apaid that I suffered for thee?" I said: "Ya good lord, gramercy. Ya, good lord, blessed may thou be." Then said Jesus, our good lord: "If thou art satisfied, I am satisfied. It is a joy, a bliss, an endless liking to me that ever I suffered my passion for thee. And if I might suffer more, I would suffer more." (22:1-5.193-195)

From St. Irenaeus in the second century to St. Augustine of Hippo in the fourth century and St. Anselm of Canterbury in the eleventh (as well as during the scholastic debates of the medieval period), theologians had taught that Christ's sacrifice on the cross was the settlement of a "debt" owed to God the Father for the grave disobedience of original sin. Because no mere human being could pay such a debt, it was necessary for the Son of God to become man, suffer, and die in order to atone for the sin of Adam. At the same time, the Savior had to "buy back" humanity from the clutches of Satan with the price of his own blood. By dying on the cross, Christ "paid the debt" of original sin, made complete satisfaction to divine justice, restored humanity to the image and likeness of God, and overcame the power of evil.[12]

Given this deeply embedded theological context, it is all the more astounding that Julian hears Christ ask her, pointedly: "Art *thou* well apaid?" He is implying that by dying on the cross, he intended to make restitution *to sinners* for the terrible suffering

---

[12]See Rolf, *Julian's Gospel*, "Atonement Theory," 304-6; "Sin as Bondage" and "Christ's Victory," 322-25; and "Adoption," 360-62. See also Hide, *Gifted Origins*, 109-14, 201.

caused by their own sins. It is obvious from the way Julian stammers repeatedly to say, "Ya, good lord, gramercy," that she herself was astounded by Christ's question. She simply cannot fathom the Lord's eager concern to know if he has done enough to show her his love. Even more, Julian hears Christ tell her that if *she* is satisfied, then *he* is satisfied—as if he was waiting for her full approval. He even adds that if he *could* have suffered more, he *would* have suffered more.

From this startling locution, Julian is given profound insight into "the mind of Christ" that she had desired. In an interior voice, Jesus tells her why he endured his passion and death: to prove his love and compassion for the suffering of human beings. Yes, sin is a grave offense against the law and the love of God. Yes, it must be atoned for by suffering. But God does not *cause* that suffering; we bring it on ourselves. According to the natural consequences of actions that are contrary to the divine law of love, every sin against the goodness and justice of God produces a comparable form of suffering. If we lie, we will be lied to. If we cheat, we will be cheated. If we hurt another, we will be hurt ourselves. If we betray, we will be betrayed. If we erupt in anger and violence, we will experience anger and violence. If we "take the sword [we] will perish by the sword" (Mt 26:52). That's the way the moral universe works. Far from demanding our suffering, the Father sent his only Son to suffer and die out of *compassion* for what we have to suffer. The implications of this revelation are vast: by taking on our flesh and blood, Christ took on our sin and our suffering. He learned what human beings have to endure because of sin. Because "he humbled himself and became obedient to the point of death— even death on a cross" (Phil 2:8), now every physical pain, every emotional upheaval, every spiritual conflict acquires redemptive meaning. Everything may be suffered in union with Christ for our own salvation and that of the whole world. Now we may be *seker* that everything will be transformed by Christ's own suffering into his eternal glory.

Are We Satisfied?

Are we able to hear Jesus ask if we are "well apaid"—that is, completely satisfied—by his joyful sacrifice for us? Do we believe that Christ is so deeply compassionate toward our own personal sufferings? Can we accept, as Julian learned to do, that "it is God's will that we have true delight with him in our salvation, and that we be mightily comforted and strengthened therein" (23:11-12.199)?

A JULIAN GEM

For we are his bliss, for in us he delights without end, and so shall we in him with his grace. All that he has done for us, and does, and ever shall, was never cost nor charge to him nor might be, but only that he did it in our humanity, beginning at the sweet incarnation, and lasting to the blessed resurrection on Easter morrow. (23:13-17.199)

▸ ▸ ▸ **THE TENTH REVELATION** ◂ ◂ ◂

Lo, How I Loved Thee!

With an expression of pure joy, Jesus looked down from the cross toward his right side and led Julian through the gaping wound into his Sacred Heart. "And there he shewed a fair, delectable place, and large enough for all mankind that shalle be saved to rest in peace and in love" (24:1-4.201).

Lest we become too literal about such an intimate and graphic image, it is important to distinguish between Christ's *physical* heart, which was pierced by a spear and which poured out blood and water, and his *divine* heart, the symbol of Christ's "endless love that was without beginning, and is, and shall be forever" (24:10.201). Julian was invited to enter into that incomparable love.[13]

A JULIAN GEM

And with this, our good lord said full blissfully: "Lo, how I loved thee," as if he had said: "My darling, behold and see thy lord, thy God, that is thy maker and thy endless joy. See thine own brother, thy savior. My child, behold and see what delight and bliss I have in thy salvation, and for my love enjoy it with me." (24:11-14.203)

---

[13]The anonymous monastic author of the thirteenth century *Ancrene Riwle* counseled anchoresses to take refuge in the wounds of Christ against every temptation: "Name Jesus often, and invoke the aid of his passion, and implore him by his sufferings, and by his precious blood, and by his death on the cross. Fly into his wounds; creep into them with thy thought. They are all open. He loved us much who permitted such cavities to be made in him, that we might hide ourselves in them. And, with his precious blood, ensanguine thine heart." *The Ancrene Riwle*, ed. and trans. James Morton (London: Camden Society, 1853; digitized as a Google ebook from Oxford University), part 4, 293.

▶ ▶ ▶ **THE ELEVENTH REVELATION** ◀ ◀ ◀

Wilt Thou See Her?

Then Julian saw Jesus look further down to the right side, which recalled to her where his blessed mother had stood at the foot of the cross (as in many medieval frescoes, paintings, and carved wooden depictions of the crucifixion).

> And with this same expression of mirth and joy, our good lord looked down on the right side, and brought to my mind where our lady stood at the time of his passion, and said: "Wilt thou see her?" And in this sweet word, it was as if he had said: "I know well that thou wouldst see my blessed mother, for after myself she is the highest joy that I might shew thee, and the most pleasure and worshippe to me. And she is most desired to be seen of all my blessed creatures." (25:1-6.203)

Christ's mother was greatly venerated and loved by medieval Christians and considered to be the most compassionate and effective mediatrix between sinners and her son. Julian must have had a deep devotion to Christ's mother because when he said the words, "Wilt thou see her?" Julian answered eagerly, "Ye good lord, gramercy. Ye good lord, if it be thy will" (25:18-20.205). She admitted that she had often prayed for such a grace and now she really expected she would be granted a vision of Mary "in bodily likeness," just as she saw Christ on the cross: "But I saw her not so" (25:21.205). Instead, Julian was granted "a ghostly sight of her" (25:21.205); that is, an *imaginative* vision.

> Just as I had seen her before little and simple, just so he shewed her then exalted and noble and glorious and pleasing to him above all creatures. And so he wills that it be known that all those who delight in him should delight in her, and in the delight that he has in her and she in him. (25:21-25.205)

In asking if Julian would like to see his blessed mother, it seemed to her that Christ was also implying, "Wilt thou see in her how much *thou* art loved? For thy love I have made her so high, so noble, so worthy. And this delights me and so I will that it does thee" (25:13-14.205, emphasis added). In this tender revelation of Christ's love for his mother, Julian understood how much he loves every single human being, as if all were only one person.

Julian notes that "our lord shewed me nothing individually but our lady Saint Mary. And he shewed her three times: the first was as she conceived; the second was as she was in her sorrows under the cross; and the third was as she is now, in delight, honor, and joy" (25:31-34.205).

▶ ▶ ▶ **THE TWELFTH REVELATION** ◀ ◀ ◀

I It Am!

Now Julian is privileged to see our Lord "more glorified as to my sight than I saw him before" (26:1-2.207). She is taught that the soul shall never have rest until it comes into God, since God alone is the fullness of all joy: "homely and courteous and blissful and full of true life" (26:3-4.207).

> Oftentimes our lord Jesus said: "I it am, I it am. I it am that is highest. I it am that thou lovest. I it am that thou likest. I it am that thou servest. I it am that thou longest for. I it am that thou desirest. I it am that thou meanest. I it am that is all. I it am that holy church preacheth to thee and teacheth thee. I it am that shewed myself before to thee." (26:4-8.207)

This magnificent litany assures Julian that Christ is the only one who can satisfy her longing to praise, love, like, serve, long for, and desire, and the only one who can give meaning to her whole life and be her "all."[14] He is also the one that holy church preaches and teaches. And the Lord affirms that it is he, and he alone, who has revealed himself to her.

> The number of the words [Christ spoke] passes my wits and my understanding and all my powers, for they were in the highest number, as to my sight. For therein is comprehended I cannot tell what. But the joy that I saw in the shewing of them surpasses all that heart can think or soul may desire. And therefore these words are not declared here. (26:8-12.207)

Previously, Julian had conveyed Christ's presence as clothing that embraces and encloses us out of love; as the goodness of all things,

---

[14]In Middle English, the verb *like* expressed even more intimacy than *love*. Julian understood that Christ wants us to "like" what he is accomplishing in us and for us.

even a humble hazelnut; as the still "point" in the center of all that is; as pure Being. She was invited by Christ to "see, I am God" (11:42.165), leading everything and everyone to the glorious end for which they were created. Now Christ reveals so many divine names that are "above every name" (Phil 2:9) that Julian finds herself at a loss to understand or repeat them all. She can only bear witness to the indescribable joy she experienced in realizing, as did St. John the Evangelist, that "all things came into being through him, and without him not one thing came into being" (Jn 1:3). For Julian, "I it am" is the love within the Trinity that encompasses all creation.

Julian is hopeful that everyone, according to God's grace, will receive these words in whatever way the Lord has spoken them to each one of us, personally. What do they mean for you?

Alle Shalle Be Wele

Following this exaltation, Julian was led by the Lord to remember the "wound of willful longing" (2:35.129) for God that she had requested so many years ago:

> And after this, our lord brought to my mind the longing that I had for him before. And I saw that nothing letted me but sinne. And so I beheld this generally in us all, and it seemed to me: "If sinne had not been, we should all have been as clean and like to our lord as he made us." And thus in my folly before this time, often I wondered why, by the great foreseeing wisdom of God, the beginning of sinne was not letted. For then I thought that alle would have been wele. (27:1-6.207-209)

She realizes that the only thing that prevents her from being fully united to God is sin. She confesses, quite candidly, that she had often thought that everything would have been well in the world *if only* God had not "allowed" sin. She admits that "this stirring was much to be rejected, but nevertheless I mourned and sorrowed over it, lacking reason and discretion" (27:7.209). Christ gently but firmly corrects her wrong view.

A JULIAN GEM

But Jesus, who in this vision informed me of all that I needed, answered by this word and said: "Sinne is behovely, but alle shalle be wele, and alle shalle be wele, and alle manner of thing shalle be wele." (27:8-11.209)

Here is certainly the most famous quotation from Julian's *Revelations*. However, most of the time you only read or hear the "alle shalle be wele" part—not the crucial "Sinne is behovely, *but*" that precedes it. By calling sin "behovely," Christ teaches Julian that sin may be "useful" and sometimes "necessary" to bring us to our knees and make us realize our need of forgiveness. Taken further, *behovely* may even mean "advantageous" in the sense that the *Exsultet*, that ancient hymn of praise sung at the Easter Vigil, suggests: "O truly necessary sin of Adam, destroyed completely by the Death of Christ! O happy fault, that earned so great, so glorious a Redeemer!"[15] Throughout this revelation, Christ is not undermining the human scourge of sin but reassuring Julian (and all of us) that "alle shalle be wele" *in spite of* sin, and on an entirely different plane of existence. St. Paul insisted, "We know that all things work together for good for those who love God, who are called according to his purpose" (Rom 8:28). St. Augustine wrote, "[God] can bring good even out of evil."[16] This is because of Christ's perfect sacrifice that triumphed over sin and death.

However, Julian can't quite accept it. She recognizes that all the pain she has experienced in her life and all the suffering she has seen around her are the result of human sinfulness. The agony she has witnessed Christ suffer on the cross was solely because of sin. How could sin ever be *behovely*?

> In this naked word "sinne," our lord brought to my mind all that is not good and the shameful contempt and the utter noughting that he bore for us in this life, and his dying, and all the pains and passions of all his creatures, spiritual and bodily. (27:11-14.209)

---

[15]"The Exsultet: The Proclamation of Easter," available at United States Conference of Catholic Bishops, www.usccb.org/prayer-and-worship/liturgical-year/easter/easter-proclamation-exsultet.cfm.

[16]St. Augustine, *The Augustine Catechism: The Enchiridion on Faith, Hope and Love*, translated by Bruce Harbert (Hyde Party, NY: New City Press, 1999), #11, 41.

We must be very clear: Julian's mental anguish about the collective and individual suffering caused by sin is not just a medieval preoccupation. Julian's confusion represents the innate sense we all have that our world is terribly broken and we don't know how to fix it. We simply cannot save ourselves from the messes we get into through our harmful actions because our ingrained patterns, our spiritual ignorance, and our moral blindness prevent us from fully understanding what is wrong. We are helpless to save ourselves.

Julian reveals that she was shown the history of suffering in the world "in a touch, and readily passed over into comfort" (27:20-21.209). However, she did not see "sinne" because she believed "it hath no manner of substance, nor no part of being; nor may it be known except by the pain that it causes" (27:22-23.211-213). But this pain eventually enables us to plead for mercy and be purged of our sinfulness. All the while, our Lord comforts us "readily and sweetly, meaning thus" (27:27.211):

> "It is true that sinne is the cause of all this pain, but alle shalle be wele, and all manner of thing shalle be wele." These words were shewn full tenderly, shewing no manner of blame to me, nor to none that shalle be saved. Then it would be a great unkindness of me to blame or wonder at God for my sinne, since he blames me not for sinne. (27:28-32.211)

With these words, Julian intuited a high and marvelous secret hidden in God, which will only be revealed to those who "shalle be saved."[17] It will show why God "allowed" sin to come into the world, "in which sight we shall endlessly have joy" (27:35-36.211).

---

[17]In the first revelation, Julian wrote, "I speak of them that shalle be saved, for in this time God shewed me nobody else. But in all things I believe as holy church teaches" (9:16-17.155-57). Decades later, from her understanding of the parable of the lord and the servant, Julian no longer differentiated between "them that shalle be saved" and the rest of humanity, believers from nonbelievers. She perceived that there was *no essential separation* between one man (or woman) and another; "For in the sight of God, all men are one man, and one man is all men" (51:88-89.279). See also Eph 2:13-22.

While Julian never denies God's sovereign right to judge and even possibly to condemn sinners for their sin, she writes only what she saw and heard; namely, that she did not see sin, divine blame, or everlasting punishment. Quite the contrary: "Thus I saw how Christ *has compassion on us* because of sinne" (28:1.211, emphasis added). This, in turn, fills Julian with great compassion for all her *evencristens* who, like herself, suffer the effects of sin. "And then I saw that each natural compassion that man hath for his evencristen with charity, it is Christ in him" (28:17-18.213). According to Julian, Christ wants us to know that, because of his own passion, all our sufferings will be turned to honors and the great profit of our souls; that we never suffer alone but always along with him; and that in his great courtesy "he takes away all our blame, and beholds us with compassion and pity as children, innocent and not loathsome" (28:28-30.213).

Julian's Question

Remarkably, even after all these reassuring insights, Julian still did not understand how all might be well:

> But in this I stood [my ground], contemplating generally, anxiously, and mournfully, saying thus to our lord in my meaning with the greatest dread: "Ah, good lord, *how* might alle be wele for the great harm that has come by sinne to thy creatures?" And here I desired, as far as I dared, to have some more open teaching wherewith I might be eased in this. (29:1-5.213-215, emphasis added)

Christ was not at all offended by Julian's insistent questioning. With a loving expression, he answered that "Adam's sinne was the most harm that ever was done or ever shalle [be done] to the world's end" (29:6-7.215). Yet Christ did not want her to focus on that (or any other) devastating sin, but rather behold his own glorious atonement, which is more pleasing to God and gives more worship than ever Adam's sin was harmful. The Lord wants us to take heed of this: "For since I have made wele the greatest harm, then it is my will that thou know thereby that I shall make wele alle that is less" (29:13-14.215). In other words, no sin is too terrible to be forgiven by the love and mercy of God (or too trite not to *need* forgiveness).

Christ's Answer

Deep within her soul, Julian heard a glorious locution concerning the ways in which Christ makes all things well.

> And thus our good lord answered to all the questions and doubts that I might make, saying very comfortingly: "I may make alle thing wele, and I can make alle thing wele, and I wille make alle thing wele, and I shalle make all thing wele. And thou shalt see thyself that alle manner of thing shalle be wele." (31:1-4.217)[18]

Jesus reveals five distinct ways in which he makes "alle thing wele." First, because he is Divine Power, Christ *may* do it in the sense that he is able to do all that needs to be done. Second, because he is Divine Wisdom, Christ *can* do it, which implies that he knows how to accomplish it. Third, because it is the Father's wish, Christ *will* do it because he chooses to do so. Fourth, since it is Christ's own intention to make everything well, he *shall* do it. And fifth, because he wants to comfort her, Christ promises Julian that she shall *see* herself that "alle manner of thing shalle be wele." Julian further understands that where Christ says "I may," that indicates the Father; where he says "I can," that is the Son; and where he says "I will," that is the Holy Ghost; and by the "I shall," that is the unity of the Blessed

---

[18]Since the Middle English *wele* was a form of *weal*, it meant not only "well," but the greatest possible happiness and "well-*being*." Also, *shalle* in Middle English conveyed much stronger intent than *will*.

Trinity. Finally, where Christ says, "Thou shalt see thyself," she understood "the oneing of all mankind that shalle be saved into the blissful trinity" (31:9.219).

"Therefore this is his thirst: *a love-longing* to have us all together, whole in him to his endless bliss, as to my sight" (31:14-16.219, emphasis added). Christ's love-longing is like that of a parent who stands watch at the window, expectantly waiting to have all the children arrive back home at last, safe and sound. Julian further acknowledges that God is continually "making well" not only the noblest and the greatest things, but also the least little things. Nothing will be forgotten.

Yet Julian laments that "there are many evil deeds done in our sight and such great harms suffered, that it seems to us that it would be unpossible that it ever could come to a good end" (32:8-9.221). Why can't we see evil deeds being made well? "And the cause is this: that the use of our reason is now so blind, so low and so simple, that we can not know the high, marvelous wisdom, the might, and the goodness of the blissful trinity" (32:11-13.221). Furthermore, we are burdened by sin, which is "the sharpest scourge that any chosen soul may be smitten with" (39:1.239). But Julian affirms that "by contrition we are made clean, by compassion we are made ready, and by true longing for God we are made worthy" (39:20-22.241). As we are purified by suffering, we will develop the minds and hearts to see how all things are being made well—in an *ultimate* sense.

> ▸ ▸ ▸ **THE FOURTEENTH REVELATION** ◂ ◂ ◂

Prayer, a Parable, and the Motherhood of God

The fourteenth revelation is the longest of all, inasmuch as it encompasses Christ's teachings on prayer; Julian's understanding of the two domes or forms of judgment; her insights on the working of mercy and grace; the account of her intense struggle to understand how God sees us in our sinfulness; her magnificent exegesis on the parable of the lord and the servant; her intuition of the godly will; and finally, her glorious mystical theology of the motherhood of God. In the Long Text, this fourteenth revelation covers *twenty-two* chapters, some of them very long. Here, indeed, is the fruit not only of all the original revelations, but also of the ongoing teachings Julian received from the Lord for twenty years after the visions had ceased.

At the beginning of this fourteenth revelation, Julian revealed what Christ taught her about prayer. She saw that there are two essential aspects of prayer. The first is the right attitude, praying only for what is God's will and to his greater worship. The second is "seker trust" (41:2.247).

> But yet oftentimes our trust is not full. For we are not seker that God hears us, and we think [it] is because of our unworthiness, and because we feel nothing at all. For we are as barren and as dry oftentimes after our prayers as we were before. And so, in our feeling, our folly is the cause of our weakness. For thus have I felt in myself. (41:3-6.247)

What insight this passage offers into Julian's own life of prayer. We can easily identify with her feeling of not being heard, or feeling unworthy, or not feeling anything at all.

A JULIAN GEM

And all this our lord brought suddenly to my mind, and shewed these words and said: "I am the ground of thy beseking. First it is my will that thou have it, and next I make thee to will it, and next I make thee to beseke it—and thou besekest it! How should it then be that thou shouldst not have thy beseking?" (41:7-10.249)

Christ taught Julian that he himself is the foundation and prime mover of prayer. First, in his great goodness, he wills to give Julian some special grace. Then he makes her desire it. Next, he inspires her to *beseke* it. Then, she actually does seek it fervently through prayer. So how could it be that she would not receive what she was looking for so earnestly, since it was Christ's will that she have it? Thus Julian understood that true prayer is not initiated by us; it is inspired by God. Prayer does not "convince" God to give us what we need—it is the means by which we are able to receive the graces that God already longs to give us. Julian felt "a mighty comfort" in being shown that the Lord himself is the ground of our prayer (41:11-12.249).

> For it is the most unpossible that may be that we should seek mercy and grace and not have it. For every thing that our good lord makes us beseke, he himself has ordained it to us from without beginning. (41:15-18.249)

Julian intuits that Christ himself receives every prayer and safeguards it in a spiritual treasury that benefits us on earth and will be a source of great joy in heaven. Through the graces we receive in prayer, we become more Christlike; and since the Lord dearly wants us to be restored to the image and likeness of God, he urges Julian (and us):

> "Pray wholeheartedly: though thou think it savour thee not, yet it is profitable enough, though thou feel it nought. Pray wholeheartedly, though thou feel nought, though thou see nought, yea,

though thou think thou might not [have any strength]. For in dryness and barrenness, in sickness and in feebleness, then is thy prayer fully pleasant to me, though thou think it savour thee not but little. And so is all thy living prayer in my sight." (41:33-38.251)

Julian adds that because Christ longs to give us rich rewards and endless thanks, he is actually "covetous" to have us pray often so that he may reward and thank us! She is certain that, no matter how dry or dull prayer may sometimes feel to us, "God accepts the good will and the travail of his servants" (41:40.251). Christ also cautions us to be "reasonable with discretion" (41:42.251), not wearing ourselves out with endless repetitions of the same prayers as if we thought the Lord did not know what we need before we ask.

In addition to the prayer of petition, Julian considers the prayer of thanksgiving as "a true, inward knowing, with great reverence and lovely awe," whereby we offer all our efforts and energies to the daily tasks that are God's will for us, all the while "rejoicing and thanking inwardly" (41:45-47.251). Notice that Julian stresses the importance of *rejoicing* in the good works we are enabled to do by the grace of God. Not only that, but she declares that our prayer and our trust should never be timid, but "both alike large," which in Middle English suggests ample and even ambitious: "For if we do not trust as much as we pray, we do not give the fullest worshippe to our lord in our prayer, and also we hinder and trouble ourselves" (42:12-13.253). We must constantly remind ourselves that "our Lord is the ground in whom our prayer springs" and that prayer is itself "given to us by grace of his love"; then we will be able to trust that we will receive "all that we desire" (42:14-16.253).

Discouragement in Prayer

Ah, but what about those times when we pray earnestly and do not get an answer? Julian knows exactly how we feel and offers some sound advice:

But sometimes it comes to our mind that we have prayed a
long time, and yet we think that we have not received what we
asked for. But therefore we should not become depressed, for
I am seker by our lord's meaning that either we must wait for
a better time, or more grace, or a better gift. He wills that we
have true knowing in himself that *he is being.* And in this
knowing, he wills that our understanding be grounded with
all our strength, and all our intention, and all our meaning.
And in this ground, he wills that we make our [dwelling] place
and our wonning. (42:19-25.253, emphasis added)

Julian is certain that our Lord has a perfectly good reason for the
delay. Perhaps there will be a better time to receive the gift; now
may not be the right time. Or perhaps the gift we want is not the
one that will satisfy our deepest desires and make us truly happy.
How often have we prayed for something we thought we could not
live without, and then, months or years later, realized what a
blessing it was that we did not receive it? Julian is certain that the
longer we persevere in prayer, the more receptive we will become
to the outpouring of divine grace. We will develop greater trust in
God's own desire for our fulfillment. We may begin to intuit that
the Lord has a much better gift in mind than anything we could ever
have imagined. Indeed, if we understand that God is not "a" being,
but the totality of Divine Being, the ground and source of all that
truly is, then we may begin to dwell *sekerly* in this sacred ground in
the changing circumstances of our lives. We may also grow more
confident when we pray for love and mercy for ourselves and for all
humankind, that it is Christ's own Spirit who prays within us.
Moreover, if we recall all the great deeds that the Lord has performed in times past, we will take heart and give thanks for the
hidden ways in which he is *werking* right now, even though we
cannot yet see it happening.

Forms of Prayer

For Julian, the whole point of prayer is that it "oneth the soul to God" (43:1.255) and enables us to want what God wants—even more than our own will. When, in those special moments, the Lord makes his presence known to the soul by a special grace, then "we have what we desire" (43:16.257). In such times of contemplative prayer, we no longer know what to pray for. Our needs and fears fall away, all spiritual striving abates, and the soul wishes only to rest in the stillness and silence of beholding God: "And this is a high, unperceivable prayer, as to my sight" (43:18.257). Within this state of mystical prayer, the soul enjoys "reverent fear, and such great sweetness and delight in him that we cannot pray at all except as he leads us to pray for the time" (43:20-21.257). Julian adds that the more the soul beholds God in this pure, contemplative prayer, "the more it desires him by grace" (43:22.257).

However desirable, Julian acknowledges that this type of "beholding" of God is not always possible. So then we must have recourse to a different kind of prayer to make the soul more "supple," one that is more active and verbal:

> For when a soul is tempted, troubled, and left to itself by unrest then is it time to pray to make itself supple and obedient to God. But the soul by no manner of prayer makes God supple to itself. For he is ever unchanging in love. And thus I saw that when we see a need for which we pray, then our lord God follows us, helping our desire. And when we of his special grace plainly behold him, seeing no other needs, then we follow him, and he draws us into him by love. (43:27-30.257)

Julian knew only too well that in times of emotional or spiritual conflicts, in times of fatigue, and when there is so much to do in our outer lives, it can become almost impossible to let go of our inner turmoil and be still, to rest peacefully in the contemplation of God.

Yet Julian insists that it is at precisely such times that we should pray for help in making the soul more pliable and receptive to divine grace. Julian cautions that we must never try to bend God's will to our own (which would be impossible anyway). Rather, we must seek to be open to whatever God is doing in the specific circumstances. All the while, we must remain confident that, as St. Paul assures us, Christ's Spirit "helps us in our weakness; for we do not know how to pray as we ought, but that very Spirit intercedes with sighs too deep for words" (Rom 8:26).

A JULIAN GEM

And thus we shall, with his sweet grace, in our own meek, continual prayer come into him now in this life by many private touchings of sweet, ghostly sights and feelings, measured to us as our simplicity may bear it. And this is wrought and shall be wrought by the grace of the holy ghost, until we shall die in longing for love. (43:36-39.257-259)

The Two Domes

Julian introduces her understanding of two "domes." In Middle English, "dome" meant judgment. It was related to "domesday" or the Day of Judgment. Here, Julian considers two distinct forms of judgment. The first dome is that of God, who judges human beings according to our "natural *substance*" or created essence; that is, in terms of medieval theology, our divinely-given capacities to reason and to will. This "substance" is good and "ever kept one in [God], whole and safe without end, and that dome is of his rightfullehede" (45:1-2.259). Divine judgment is not at all to be feared, for it flows from God's "own high, endless love" (45:11-12.261). And it was "that fair, sweet dome that was shewn in all the fair revelation, in which I saw him [Christ] assign to us no manner of blame" (45:12-13.261).

The second dome is that of humankind, judging us on the basis of our "changeable *sensuality*, which seems now one way and now another" (45:3.261, emphasis added). This "sensuality" refers not to the sexual desires and needs of the body but to the lower faculties of the soul, ever conflicted between "godly" and "beastly" impulses. Sensuality limits the soul as considered in its fallen state. Julian describes this lower judgment of our nature as "mixed, for sometimes it is good and easy, and sometimes it is hard and grievous" (45:4-5.261). Just as Julian was shown the higher dome throughout all of the "fair revelation" and firmly believed she must accept it, so the lower dome had always been taught to her by holy church and therefore she refused to abandon it.

Julian's Struggle

Herein lies Julian's conflict: even though she was certain that she saw "no manner of blame" in the judgment of Christ, she admits that she "could not be fully eased" (45:14.261) because she was ever mindful of the earthly judgment of the church, which taught that she must consider herself a sinner. As a devout Christian, Julian could not discount the gravity of sin and the necessity of punishment for wrong deeds, whether by suffering here on earth or after death, in purgatory or in hell. She readily acknowledges that she was never tempted to give up the teachings of the church on sin and restitution; in fact, she "had teaching to love it and like it" (46:19.263). She freely admits "that we are sinners and do many evils that we ought to leave, and leave many good deeds undone that we ought to do, wherefore we deserve pain, blame, and wrath" (46:21-23.263). Nevertheless, Julian could not deny the truth of her revelation that God is "never wroth" and assigns "no manner of blame" to sinners.

And notwithstanding all this, I saw truthfully that our lord was never wroth nor never shall be. For he is God, he is good, he is truth, he is love, he is peace. And his might, his wisdom, his charity, and his unity do not permit him to be wroth. For I saw truly that it is against the property of his might to be wroth, and against the property of his wisdom, and against the property of his goodness. God is that goodness that may not be wroth, for God is nothing but goodness. (46:24-29.263)

As powerful as this revelation was to Julian, she felt deeply torn between the two "domes" or forms of judgment—that of God and of the church—that seemed incompatible. At the same time, she was convinced that both had been revealed by God and both must somehow be "saved" and firmly believed. How could this be done? Julian's struggle was not only theological, it was deeply spiritual. She had seen so many evil deeds and atrocities committed in her lifetime; she had heard countless stories about the brutalities of war; she knew about the excommunication and damning of heretics; she remembered those who had died unshriven during the plagues. She could not shy away from confronting the dichotomy between the unconditional love of Christ toward sinners and the harsh, judgmental condemnations of sinners that she had heard preached from the pulpit. It became essential to her peace of mind to know whether sinners are really judged and condemned by the higher dome of God as they are by the lower dome of the church.

Mercy and Grace

Hitherto, Julian had been taught that "the mercy of God should be the forgiveness of his wrath after the time that we have sinned" (47:5-7.265). She had considered that for a person whose lifelong desire and purpose was to love, "the wrath of God would be harder than any other pain" (47:8.265). As a result, she had always assumed "that the forgiveness of his wrath should be one of the main aspects of his mercy" (47:8-9.265). However, now that she has realized there is "no wrath in God," she needs to reconsider the working of divine mercy. Essentially, "if God is not 'wroth,' how can he forgive?"[19]

> I understood thus: Man is changeable in this life, and by frailty and ignorance falls into sinne. He is powerless and foolish in himself, and also his will is corrupted at this time [by sinne]. He is in turmoil and in sorrow and woe. And the cause is blindness, for he does not see God. For if he saw God continually, he would have no mischievous feeling, nor no manner of stirring, nor sorrowing that inclines to sin. (47:13-17.265)

While Julian admits our common experience of changeability, frailty, and ignorance in this life, she knows that it is not the full picture because it does not take into account "the great desire that the soul hath to see God" (47:20-21.265). This, in turn, leads her to reflect on the divine work of mercy that the Holy Spirit is forever accomplishing in us, dwelling in our soul, *sekerly* keeping us, bringing us to a greater peace, making us more obedient, more pliant, and reconciling us to God whenever we become angry.

> *For I saw no wrath but on humanity's part, and that God forgives in us.* For wrath is nothing else but a rebelliousness and a contrariousness to peace and to love. And either it comes from failure of strength, or from failure of wisdom, or from failure of goodness, *which failing is not in God but is on our own part.* For we by sin and wretchedness have in us a wrath and a continuing contrariousness to peace and to love, and

---

[19]Nicholas Watson and Jacqueline Jenkins, eds., *The Writings of Julian of Norwich: A Vision Showed to a Devout Woman and A Revelation of Love* (University Park: The Pennsylvania State University Press, 2006), 264.

that he shewed very often in his loving chere of compassion
and pity. (48:5-8.267, emphasis added)

Julian understands that God intervenes in our own wrathfulness
and *contrariousness* to show us mercy: "For the ground of mercy is
in love, and the werking of mercy is our protection in love" (48:10-
11.267). And sometimes God's work of mercy even allows us to fall,
within limits, which feels to us like dying. But in that dying, we
realize all the more truly that God is our life. "Our failing is dreadful,
our falling is shameful, and our dying is sorrowful. But yet in all this
the sweet eye of pity and love never departs from us, nor does the
werking of mercy ever cease" (48:19-22:267).

Thus Julian beheld the property of mercy and the property of grace
as working together in the super-abundance of Christ's compassion
and love. Mercy belongs to "motherhood in tender love" and grace
belongs to "royal lordship in the same love" (48:24, 25.267), like two
devoted parents who function in perfect harmony. "And grace
werketh with mercy" (48:27.267), raising us up from our misdeeds
and even rewarding us (eternally surpassing what our love and our
service could possibly deserve), showing us the "plenteous largesse
of God's royal lordship in his marvelous courtesy" (48:29.269). This
divine mercy and grace are poured out on us "to slake and waste our
wrath" (48:40-41.269). In other words, far from being wrathful
toward us, God helps us let go of our own self-hatred and anger, and
teaches us to forgive one another. Julian even dares to suggest that
"our lord God, with respect to himself, *may not forgive*, for he may not
be wroth. It were unpossible" (49:2-3.269, emphasis added).

Julian realizes that if God were to be "wroth a touch"—that is, angry
even for a little while—"we should neither have life, nor place, nor
being" (49:13-14.269). We would be wiped out of existence. Have we
ever taken time to consider this? God's *unconditional love* is a much
more demanding belief than divine wrathfulness. The realization that

we are always loved, no matter what, is such an overwhelming experience that it humbles and purifies the soul more perfectly than any shame or punishment ever could. We begin to understand, like Julian, that Christ hung on the cross not because God's wrath had to be appeased, but because God's love had to be revealed.

A JULIAN GEM

For this was shown: that our life is all grounded and rooted in love, and without love we may not live. And therefore, to the soul that because of his special grace sees so deeply into the high, marvelous goodness of God, and sees that we are endlessly oned to him in love, it is the most unpossible that may be that God should be wrath. (49:3-7.269)

Julian's Plea

In spite of the sublime illuminations she has been receiving, Julian feels increasing conflict and confusion. She dares to ask the Lord for greater clarity:

> But yet here I wondered and marveled with all the diligence of my soul, meaning thus: "Good lord, I see that thou art very truth, and I know truly that we sin grievously all day and are much blameworthy. And I may neither abandon the knowing of this truth, nor can I not see the shewing [Christ has made] to us of no manner of blame. How may this be?" (50:5-9.271)

Essentially, she is being pulled between two strongly held beliefs: on the one hand, the lack of wrath and blame in God, and on the other hand, the teaching of the church that God condemns sinners.

> And between these two contraries, my reason was greatly afflicted by my blindness and could have no rest, for dread that

his blessed presence would pass from my sight and I would
be left in unknowing *how he beholds us in our sinne.* For
either it behooved me to see in God that sinne was completely done away with, or else it behooved me to see in God
how he sees it, whereby I might truly know how it is fitting
for me to see sinne and the manner of our blame. (50:14-
19.273, emphasis added)

This is such a crucial moment in Julian's revelations. Let us try to
place ourselves in her state of mental and emotional conflict:

My longing endured, while I was continually beholding him
[Christ]. And yet I could have no patience for my great fear and
perplexity, thinking: "If I take it thus, that we are *not* sinners
nor *not* blameworthy, it seems as if I should err and fail in
knowing of this truth. And if it be true that we *are* sinners and
are blameworthy, good lord, how may it then be that *I can not
see this truth in thee,* who art my God, my maker, in whom I
desire to see all truth?" (50:19-24.273, emphasis added)

It is clear that Julian was deeply troubled that in her human ignorance of such exalted teachings she would be unable to accept both
aspects of the revelation at once; she might cling to one and reject
the other and thus fall into heresy. However, she took courage in that
her request for clarity was "so low a thing; for if it were one high, I
should be afraid" (50:25-26.273). Indeed, she was not questioning
Christian doctrine; she simply wanted to know how she should view
sin and salvation. At the same time, she knew that she was not asking
for a private revelation because her question about how God sees us
in our sin was a general one that affected all her *evencristens.* She
considered that if she were to live after her revelations ceased, she
needed to have a greater "knowing of good and evil" so that she
might, "by reason and by grace, better separate them in two, and
love goodness and hate evil as holy church teaches" (50:28-29.273).

I cried inwardly with all my might, seeking into God for help, meaning thus: "Ah, lord Jesus, king of bliss, how shall I be eased? Who shall tell me and teach me what I need to know, if I may not at this time see it in thee?" (50:31-33.273)

This is not only Julian's urgent plea; it is very much our own question as well: *How does God behold us in our sin?* Are we fully saved by Christ's unconditional love, or justly condemned by our sins?

Parable of the Lord and the Servant

At the height of Julian's spiritual conflict, she is shown a parable (what medieval preachers called an *exemplum*) to answer her burning question. The parable appears in her imagination suddenly—like a short, silent film in vivid color—and features two characters, a lord and his servant. While it has only one main dramatic action, this *exemplum* contains great depth of meaning hidden in a mystical puzzle that Julian must solve. She understands that everything she sees concerning both the lord and the servant has a *double meaning*. The first level of meaning appears "ghostly in bodily likeness," played out in her imagination; the second is shown "more ghostly without bodily likeness," on a spiritual plane (51:4-5.273). It is a vivid drama, full of mystery:

The lord sits solemnly in rest and in peace. The servant stands before his lord reverently, ready to do his lord's will. The lord looks upon his servant very lovingly and sweetly, and meekly he sends him into a certain place to do his will. The servant not only goes, but suddenly he starts and runs in great haste out of love to do his lord's will. And anon he falls into a slade, and takes very great soreness. And then he groneth and moneth and walloweth and writheth. But he may not rise nor help himself by any manner of way. And in all this, the most misfortune that I saw him in was his lack of comfort. For he could not turn his face to look up on his loving lord, who was very near to him, in whom is complete comfort. But like a man that was full feeble and unwise at the time, he concentrated on his feelings and enduring in woe. In which woe he suffered seven great pains. (51:7-19.273-275)

Julian defines the servant's seven great pains as "sore bruising" (suffered from the actual fall and resulting in severe bodily injuries); "heaviness of his body" (from lying cramped in the ditch and being unable to extricate himself); "feebleness that followed on these two" (extreme weakness, both physical and spiritual); being "blinded in his reason and stunned in his mind to such an extent that he had almost forgotten his own love" (for the lord); his terrible realization that "he might not rise" (or escape from his agony); being convinced that he "lay alone," with no hope of help (there was no one to come to his aid, neither "far nor near, neither high nor low"); and finally, "the place in which he lay was a long, hard, and grievous one" (the ditch was so narrow and cramped that he could not move) (51:20-27.275).

What Julian cannot figure out is *why* the servant, who had not merely walked, but *run* off to do the lord's bidding with such eager enthusiasm, landed in the ditch, face down, so that he could not even turn his face to look upon his loving lord. She tried to discover if she could see in him any moral defect "or if the lord should assign to him any manner of blame" (51:29-30.275). But she could find nothing. "For only his good will and his great desire were the cause of his falling" (51:31.275). Indeed, the servant was "as good inwardly as he was when he stood before his lord, ready to do his will" (51:32-33.275). Julian noticed that all the time, the lord continued to behold the servant with great tenderness "and now with a double chere" (51:34.275)—that is, the lord's *outward* expression was full of compassion and pity while the lord's *inward*, more "ghostly" expression was one of rejoicing. Indeed, Julian writes that "I saw him highly enjoy the worshipful restoration and nobility that he will and must bring his servant by his plenteous grace" (51:36-38.275). How could it be that the lord would *rejoice* in his servant's fall? To add to this mysterious dichotomy, Julian understood that she must keep both aspects of the *shewing* in her mind simultaneously.

As a spiritual understanding of the lord's intention descended into her soul, Julian realized that because of the servant's fall and all the woes that came upon him as a result of that fall (and also in light of the lord's great goodness and his own honor), "his dearworthy servant, whom he loved so much, should be highly and blissfully rewarded without end, above what he should have been if he had *not* fallen" (51:47-49.275, emphasis added). She saw that the servant's "falling and all the woe that he had suffered would be turned into high, transcendent honor and endless bliss" (51:50-51.277).

Then, as suddenly as it arose, the *shewing* of the *exemplum* vanished, and Julian was left to contemplate it for the rest of her life. She admits that she could not draw any comfort from it at the time it was shown, nor did it seem to answer her question about how God sees us in our sin, at least not at first. She assumed that the servant stood for Adam, but there were so many diverse aspects of the servant (obedience, humility, goodness, and great love) that did not fit in with her idea of the imperfect Adam that "in that time I remained in great ignorance" (51:58-59.277). Notably, Julian's complete inability to comprehend the *exemplum* was such that she did not even include it in her first version of the *Revelations*, the Short Text.

A JULIAN GEM

For twenty years after the time of the shewing, save three months, I had teaching inwardly, as I shall say: "It belongeth to thee to take heed to all the properties and the conditions that were shewn in the example, though you think that it is misty or unimportant to thy sight." (51:73-76.277)

Sometimes it takes years for us to understand the deeper meaning of the Lord's revelations in our lives. In Julian's case, for nearly twenty years, she replayed in her mind all the details of the *exemplum*. Then, as advised spiritually, she "took heed" of every aspect of the parable, paying attention to the smallest details.

The Lord

Julian observed where the lord sat—not on a throne in a great hall, but "on the earth, barren and deserted, alone in the wilderness" (51:103-104.279). She remembered the azure blue color of the lord's clothing (indicating high estate and steadfast loyalty), as well as the wide, voluminous cut of his garments (that revealed he enclosed within himself all heavens in endless joy and bliss). She noted an outward expression of mercy in his beautiful pale brown face. She was struck by the lord's handsome black eyes that manifested great seriousness, "shewing full of lovely pity, and within him was a high refuge, long and broad, all full of endless heavens" (51:107-108.279). She noticed that the way the lord looked on his servant—even in his falling—"might melt our hearts for love and break them in two for joy" (51:110.279). She remarked that the look was a mixture of joy and bliss that surpassed the look of compassion and pity "as heaven is above earth" (51:113.279). While Julian issued the strong caveat that "we may not see our father God, as he is" (because "the father is not man" but is necessarily depicted figuratively and familiarly "as a man"), nevertheless she understood that the lord in the parable was meant to stand for God (51:120-123.279).

The Servant

Likewise, Julian scrutinized the servant, who she assumed was Adam: "that is to say, one man was shewn at that time, and his falling, thereby to make it understood how God beholds all mankind and his falling" (51:87-88.277-279). The servant stood at the lord's left side like a poor *villein*, or peasant farmer, who had just been hired but not yet sent out to work, although his short, white *kirtel* was already threadbare, sweaty, and ready to be ripped up for rags. Julian marveled at this disreputable-looking servant, thinking: "'This is now an unseemly clothing for the servant who is so highly loved to stand in before so honorable a lord!'" (51:145-146.281). At the same time, Julian was struck by the servant's inward "ground of love, which love he had for the lord that was even comparable to the love that the lord had for him" (51:147-148.281). The servant knew that "there was one thing to do which should be worshippe to the lord" (51:149-150.281). And so he ran to do the lord's will, with no thought of what might befall him. It seems "there was a treasure in the earth which the lord loved" (51:157.281). Julian wondered what the treasure might be. The answer came in her understanding: "It is a mete which is appealing and appetizing to the lord" (51:158-159.281). Indeed, she had noticed that the lord had neither food nor drink in the wilderness, and only one servant, whereas any great lord would have had an abundance of food and drink and many servants to do his bidding. What labor should the servant perform to produce this precious food?

> And then I understood that he [the servant] should do the greatest labor and the hardest travail that there is: he should

be a gardener: delve and dike and swinke and swete and turn the earth up and down, and seek the depnesse and water the plants in time. And in this he would continue his travail, and make sweet rivers to run, and noble and plenteous fruit to spring forth which he would bring before the lord and serve him therewith to his liking. And he should never return till he had got this mete all ready, as he knew that it was liked by the lord, and then he should take this mete with the drink, and bear it full worshippefully before the lord. And all this time the lord should sit right on the same place, awaiting the servant whom he sent out. (51:162-171.281-283)

Of course! Like the first Adam, the servant was sent out to work the soil by the sweat of his brow and bid never to return to the lord until he should bring him the precious food and drink. Julian realized that the lord contained within himself all life and goodness except this treasure "that was in the earth, and that was grounded within the lord in marvelous depnesse of endless love" (51:174-175.283). Why did the lord need this treasure? Julian perceived that until the servant brought forth this earthly treasure, the lord would not receive his fullest worship and honor. But what made the willing servant fall into the ditch? Remarkably, the cause of the servant's fall is never specified. In this *exemplum* (suggesting the fall of Adam), there is no forbidden apple and no tempting snake; nor is there any figure of Eve who, according to the church's teaching, was the cause of Adam's downfall.

Double Nature

Eventually, Julian saw into the heart of the mystery. The servant had a double nature. In his divinity he was Jesus, the Lord's beloved Son, who had never before been "sent out" in the flesh; but in his humanity he was Adam, who had been toiling and turning over the earth for generations, hence his dirty, threadbare *kirtel*. Suddenly it made perfect theological sense:

> When Adam fell, God's son fell. Because of the perfect union [of God and man] which was made in heaven, God's son might not be separated from Adam, for by Adam I understood all humankind. (51:185-187:283)

Here Julian acknowledges the ancient dogma of the "hypostatic union." According to this doctrine, the unique person of Jesus Christ has two natures, one divine and one human.

> The doctrine of the hypostatic union was affirmed at the Council of Ephesus in 431 CE. Thereafter, the relationship between the two natures of Jesus Christ, divine and human, was clarified and promulgated at the Council of Chalcedon in 451 CE.

Julian also references the medieval belief that the human nature of Jesus Christ had pre-existed in heaven before he took flesh in the womb of Mary. Thus there was never a time that Christ, the perfect creation, was not "oned" with humanity. Just as Adam, because of his sin of disobedience, "fell from life to death: into the slade of this wretched world and after that into hell," so "God's son fell with Adam into the slade of the maiden's womb, who was the fairest daughter of Adam—and that was to excuse Adam from blame in heaven and on earth—and mightily he fetched him out of hell" (51:187-191.283). Notice that "falling" has a double meaning, indicating both Adam's fall into sin and Christ's falling into the maiden's womb. Here Julian is clearly writing in universal terms because all men and all women are included in her understanding of "Adam." In taking on our human nature, Christ did not differentiate one sort of person from another. He became one with all humanity in everything save sin. At last, Julian has solved the central paradox of the parable: God the Father looks upon the servant (and all humanity) with only the most tender compassion and pity for our fallen condition, "for in all this our good lord shewed his own son and Adam *but one man*" (51:194-195.283, emphasis added).

A JULIAN GEM

And thus has our good lord Jesus taken upon himself all our blame, and therefore our father may not, nor will not, assign any more blame to us than to his own dearworthy son, Jesus Christ. (51:197-199.283)

This means that when God "looks" at humanity, God "sees" Jesus Christ. God cannot and does not *blame* us for our ignorance and sinfulness because he cannot assign blame to his own Son. On the contrary, the Father wishes only to draw all of us out of the narrow ditch of this mortal life.

Deciphering the Parable

Julian realized that the staining and tearing of the servant's *kirtel* indicated "the blows and the scourges, the thorns and the nails, the drawing and the dragging, his tender flesh tearing" of Christ's passion (51:246-248.287). And by the writhing and moaning of the servant in the ditch, she understood Christ's sufferings on the cross, from which he could not rise until he had been slain and yielded his soul into the Father's hand "with all mankind for whom he was sent" (51:253.287). Thus salvation was wrought by the "perfect" Adam, Jesus Christ, who excused the "biblical" Adam (representing all humanity) from its slavery to sin.

> Now the lord no longer sits on the earth in the wilderness, but he sits on his rich and noble seat which he made in heaven, much to his pleasure. Now the son does not stand before the father as a servant before the lord, fearfully, wretchedly clothed, partly naked, but he stands directly in front of the father, richly clothed in blissful amplitude, with a crown upon his head of precious richness. For it was shewn that "we are his crown"; which crown is the father's joy, the son's worshippe, the holy ghost's liking, and endless, marvelous bliss to all that are in heaven. (51:265-272.287)

Julian concludes her probing into the allegorical and moral layers of the *exemplum* with an eschatological realization that the Son no longer stands at the side like a poor servant, but directly in front of the Father, clothed in the full radiance of resurrected glory. He wears a crown sparkling with "precious richness" that bears witness to his triumph over sin and death. And "*we* are his crown"!

In deciphering this parable of the lord and the servant, Julian has created a work of sublime mystical art. If we are willing to take time to read and reflect on Julian's understanding of the inseparable relationship between the lord and the servant (as both Christ and Adam), we may be astounded at how God "sees us in our sinne."[20]

The Godly Will

When Julian finally understood the parable, she received a partial answer to her question about how, in the sight of God, we could be both sinners and saved, images of both the imperfect Adam and the perfect Christ. While she still harbored questions, Julian was greatly comforted by an understanding of the godly will:

> And in this that I have now said was my desire in part answered, and my great fear somewhat eased, by the lovely

---

[20]For further implications of the parable, see "The Lord and the Servant," in Rolf, *Julian's Gospel*, 462-93.

gracious shewing of our lord God. In which shewing I saw and understood full sekerly that in each soul that shall be saved is *a godly will that never assented to sinne, nor never shall*. Which will is so good that it may never will evil, but evermore continually it wills good and werks good in the sight of God. Therefore our lord wills we know it in the faith and in the belief, and specifically and truly that we have all this blessed will whole and safe in our lord Jesus Christ. (53:7-14.293, emphasis added)

The "godly will" was one of the many insights that Julian received during her decades of contemplation on the parable. She perceived that there is "a godly will that never assented to sinne, nor never shall." Earlier, Julian had marveled that even though the servant fell into the ditch, becoming feeble and ignorant, and despite the fact he could not turn his head to see his loving lord and was blinded about knowing his own will, nonetheless, "his will was kept whole in God's sight" (51:91.279). What is this godly will? To understand what Julian means, we must first examine how she describes our creation:

And thus I understood that man's soul is made of nothing. That is to say, it is created, but of nothing that is made, as thus: when God would make man's body, he took the slime of the earth, which is a matter mixed and gathered from all bodily things, and thereof he made man's body. But to the making of man's soul he would take nothing at all, but made it. And thus is the [created] nature rightfully made united to the maker who is essential nature uncreated, that is God. *And therefore it is that there may nor shall be truly nothing at all between God and man's soul.* (53:34-40.295, emphasis added)

The godly will, then, is our divinely created nature, fashioned out of nothing in the image and likeness of God (Gen 1:26). It is our *existential link* to our Creator, which may never be broken. It is the indwelling of God's will in our soul, and it is our soul's will and desire to be united with God. No one and nothing can satisfy that desire but God.

Theologically speaking, the godly will is the "higher part," or pure substance of the soul, which "wills good and werks good in the sight of God." It includes our mental capacities to be aware, to reason, to remember, and to choose the good. Unlike the "lower part" of the soul that conditions our natural appetites for food, procreation, and self-preservation, the "higher part" of the soul wills our spiritual perfection. In truth, "we are what he has made us, created in Christ Jesus for good works, which God prepared beforehand to be our way of life" (Eph 2:10). For Julian, we are not only created *good*; we are created *godly*.[21]

Of course, we may misuse and abuse our godly will. Because of sin, the rational and sensual faculties of our soul have become weakened, ignorant, easily misguided. Thus we may turn away from the eternal good for which we are created, give in to the carnal drives of our lower nature, and choose lesser goods that involve sinful behavior. Then we may fall into a ditch of darkness and despair through our "feebleness and blindness." But Julian insists that the soul that shall be saved *never fully assents* to serious sin; therefore, sin does not nullify the godly will, for it is ever kept safe and secure in the ground of our Christ-redeemed humanity.

> Wherefore, he wills we know that the noblest thing that ever he made is mankind, and the fullest substance and the highest virtue is the blessed soul of Christ. And furthermore, he wills that we know that this dearworthy soul was

---

[21]For further discussion, see "The Great Deed" and "The Godly Will," in Rolf, *Julian's Gospel*, 421-22, 494-511. See also Nuth, *Wisdom's Daughter*, 114-16, and Hide, *Gifted Origins*, 76-88, 208.

preciously knit to him in the making. Which knot is so subtle and so mighty that it is oned into God, in which oning it is made endlessly holy. Furthermore, he wills we know that all the souls that shall be saved in heaven without end are knit in this knot, and oned in this oneing, and made holy in this holiness. (53:47-54.295)

Think of it! Even when we sin, God sustains our soul's awareness (without which we would not be able to experience anything), as well as our rational ability to know and to choose the good. Even when we go astray, God continues to love us unconditionally and sends his Son to bring us back home. Moreover, because of our glorious redemption, when God "looks" at us, God sees the Beloved, with whom he is "well pleased" (Mt 3:17; Lk 3:22). This is what it means for our essential nature to be kept "whole and safe": we are inseparably knitted and *oned* to Christ.

The Motherhood of God

For some readers, Julian's teachings on the motherhood of God are the most difficult and daring of all. For others, they grow organically out of Julian's personal experience of the love and compassion of Christ on the cross.

> For the almighty truth of the trinity is our father, for he made us and keeps us in himself. And the deep wisdom of the trinity is our mother, in whom we are all enclosed. And the high goodness of the trinity is our lord, and in him we are enclosed and he in us. (54:15-18.297)

Who conceives, protects, and nurtures in a womb, out of which life is born? Who loves unconditionally and is willing to suffer anything for the sake of the child? Who forgives the child without blame? Who stoops down to comfort and protect the child in every danger?

For Julian, given the strict separation of male and female roles in her medieval world, it was *the mother*. It should be noted, however, that in our own time "maternal" care may be given by either parent, grandparents, foster parents, caregivers, teachers, spiritual guides, and so on. It's not about gender, it's about *function*: whoever nurtures a child in any way is doing the work of Christ our Mother. I have long been convinced that Julian's own experience of motherhood enabled her to write about the motherhood of God with a personal knowledge, tenderness, and conviction that radiates through her theology.

The Wisdom Tradition

In Julian's time, there was already a long biblical, monastic, and scholastic tradition of referring variously to the Father, to Christ, and to the Holy Spirit as life-generating, self-sacrificing, loving, nurturing, and disciplining.[22] The Hebrew word for wisdom (*hokmah*) and the Greek word for wisdom (*sophia*) are both feminine nouns. In the book of Proverbs, feminine Wisdom appears before anything else is created (Prov 8:22-23) and the earth is formed through the power of this life-giving Wisdom (Prov 3:19). The sublime qualities of *hokmah/sophia* are numerous and of infinite variety: "She is a breath of the power of God, and a pure emanation of the glory of the Almighty, . . . a reflection of eternal light, a spotless mirror of the working of God, and an image of his goodness" (Wis 7:25-26). Divine Wisdom was understood as the eternal nurturing figure.

Following in the Wisdom tradition, St. Anselm of Canterbury (1033–1109) prayed to Jesus as a mother who "gathers her chickens under her wings" and who dies in order to bring forth her children

---

[22]See "The Wisdom Tradition," in Rolf, *Julian's Gospel*, 512-14. See also Caroline Walker Bynum, *Jesus as Mother: Studies in the Spirituality of the High Middle Ages* (Berkeley: University of California Press, 1982), 131, 151, 187, 190-91.

in labor.[23] St. Bernard of Clairvaux (1090–1153), William of St. Thierry (1085–1148), and St. Aelred of Rievaulx (1110–1167) wrote of Jesus-as-mother to describe his compassion, his nurturing, and his profound union with the soul.[24] The scholastic writers of the twelfth and thirteenth centuries—Peter Lombard, Abelard, St. Albert the Great, St. Thomas Aquinas, and St. Bonaventure—used maternal imagery to refer to Christ as the Wisdom of God or to depict the work of the Holy Spirit. Their references speak "primarily of God as creator of life or illuminator of knowledge."[25] The thirteenth century visionary nuns of Helfta (Mechthild of Hackeborn, Mechthild of Magdeburg, and St. Gertrude the Great) considered divine motherhood to be expressive not only of God's justice and merciful love but also of authority and stern discipline.[26] And Richard Rolle, in his commentary on the first verse of the Song of Songs, imagined the breasts of Christ filled with the spiritual milk of motherly love.[27]

However, it should be noted that these various aspects of divine motherhood were described *metaphorically*. It was understood that there could be no gender in divinity, since God is pure spirit. Furthermore, in spite of occasional references to the divinity as feminine, the Hebrew Scriptures typically alluded to the all-powerful Creator and divine Judge as masculine, using the male pronoun when referencing Yahweh, Jehovah, or God. Jesus told his disciples to pray to God as "Our Father" and personally called God his "Abba" (an Aramaic form of "Daddy"). The works of medieval scholasticism also employed the masculine pronoun for God and

---

[23]St. Anselm, *Prayer to St. Paul*, from *The Prayers and Meditations of St. Anselm, with the Proslogion*, trans. Benedicta Ward (New York: Penguin, 1973), 153-56.

[24]Caroline Walker Bynum, *Jesus as Mother: Studies in the Spirituality of the High Middle Ages* (Berkeley: University of California Press, 1982), 131.

[25]Bynum, *Jesus as Mother*, 151.

[26]Ibid., 187, 190.

[27]Robert Boenig, "The God-as-Mother Theme in Richard Rolle's Biblical Commentaries," *Mystics Quarterly* 10, no. 4 (December 1984): 171-74.

medieval sermons consistently alluded to God in masculine, not feminine, terms. Thus it was daring for Julian to assign the human qualities of motherhood to God—and especially to Jesus Christ, the *Son* of God—as the foundation of her trinitarian theology.

The Process of Oneing

Julian based her reasoning in the act of conception/creation and the ongoing process of *oneing*:

> God, the blessed trinity, who is everlasting being, truly as he is endless from without beginning, so truly was it his endless purpose to make mankind; which fair human nature was first assigned to his own son, the second person. And when he wished, by full accord of all the trinity, he made us all at once. And in our making he knit us and oned us to himself, by which oneing we are kept as clean and as noble as we were made. (58:1-6.307)

God-in-Trinity created humanity "all at once," with Christ, the God-man, as its prototype. Through our individual creations, each of us is knitted and joined inseparably to Christ. Because of this process of knitting and *oneing* within the Trinity (like a babe growing in its mother's womb), "we love our maker and like him, praise him and thank him and endlessly take great joy in him" (58:8.307).

> And thus in our creation God almighty is our natural father, and God all wisdom is our natural mother, with the love and the goodness of the holy ghost, who is all one God, one lord. And in the knitting and in the oneing he is our very true spouse, and we are his beloved wife and his fair maiden, with which wife he was never displeased. For he says: "I love thee and thou lovest me, and our love shall never be separated in two." (58:9-14.307)

We have no way of knowing if Julian was acquainted with the scriptural and monastic Wisdom literature mentioned above. But it is very clear that Julian was not thinking of motherhood merely as a *metaphor* for eternal creativity and divine nurturing; nor does she speak of motherhood as a *simile*, in that Christ is "like" a mother. In Julian's theology, Jesus Christ is *literally and truly* "our very mother: we have our being from him, where the ground of motherhood begins, with all the sweet protection of love that endlessly follows" (59:7-9.309). Thus Julian establishes divine maternity as the cornerstone of her mystical theology.

Furthermore, Julian clearly implies that Christ's motherhood is perfectly equal to the divine fatherhood. As one theologian noted, for Julian "the roles of mother and father have *equal theological status.* The implications are that both masculine and feminine images are essential in describing who God is in relation to creatures."[28] Julian even goes so far as to interchange gender references for Christ. In the same sentence, she refers to Christ as "our mother," and uses the personal pronoun "he." In doing so, she greatly expands the possibilities of how we might conceive of our Creator and Redeemer.

With St. Paul, Julian realizes that in Christ "all things in heaven and on earth were created, things visible and invisible, whether thrones or dominions or rulers or powers—all things have been created through him and for him" (Col 1:16). Julian deduces that if the Son "gives birth" to everything that exists, then he must be our original and truest mother, from whom all motherhood gets its name. Julian bases her theology of divine motherhood on the fact that our Father, almighty God, who is pure being, "knew and loved us from before any time began" (59:20-21.311). And out of the fullness of that love, our Father wished that the second person of the blessed Trinity would become "our mother, our brother, and our savior" (59:23.311). Therefore, it follows that "as truly as God is our father, as truly God is our mother" (59.23-24.311).

---

[28]Kerrie Hide, *Gifted Origins to Graced Fulfillment: The Soteriology of Julian of Norwich* (Collegeville, MN: Liturgical Press, 2001), 136, emphasis added.

Julian understands three ways of beholding motherhood in God. First, God is our mother because the Creator birthed us into life. Second, Christ is our mother through the incarnation when his motherhood of grace began. Third, Christ continually works as our mother by spreading forth the length and breadth, height and depth of mercy and grace, thus bringing us back into our natural home where we were created in Trinity. Julian affirms that these three forms of divine motherhood are all "one love" (59:41.311).

Christ's Motherhood

Most poignantly, Julian expresses how much the Son of God *longed* to become our mother in the flesh as well as in spirit. That is why Christ became incarnate: "he arrayed and prepared himself in our poor flesh in the maiden's womb precisely so that he could do the service and the office of motherhood in all thing" (60:10-11.313). How does Julian describe this "office of motherhood"?

A JULIAN GEM

The mother's service is nearest, rediest, and sekerest: nearest, for it is most natural; rediest, for it is most loving; and sekerest, for it is truest. This office might not nor could ever be performed to the fullest except by him [Christ] alone. (60:12-14.313)

Here Julian reveals the many ways in which Christ is truly our mother, sharing our own human nature, ever ready to protect and help us, always reliable, stable, and trustworthy. In fact, for Julian, Christ is the *only* perfect mother. This means that all who give birth or nurture others actually acquire their "mothering" skills from Christ. Julian even claims that there is no aspect of physical pregnancy and birth that Christ did not experience: she envisions

Christ as a flesh and blood woman, carrying us in his womb throughout his earthly mission. Then, during his passion, Christ our mother went into labor with excruciating birth pangs, cries, fears, and the outpouring of blood and water from the cross, in order to give us birth. Then he *died* in childbirth, the way countless women did during Julian's lifetime. Afterward, Christ wanted to do still more for his children. Julian recalls how the Lord had told her from the cross, "If I might suffer more, I would suffer more" (60:21-22.313). Julian acknowledges that "he might not die any more, but he would not stop werking. Wherefore it behooves him to feed us, for the dearworthy love of motherhood has made him our debtor" (60:22-24.313). So, Christ continues to nurture and teach us just as a human mother feeds and instructs her child throughout the years.

There is simply no end to Christ's motherly love. With great tenderness, Julian even envisions Christ as a *nursing* mother:

> The mother may give her child to suck her milk, but our precious mother Jesus, he may feed us with himself, and does so most courteously and most tenderly with the blessed sacrament that is the precious food of true life. And with all the sweet sacraments he sustains us most mercifully and graciously. And so he meant in these blessed words where he said: "I it am that holy church preacheth [to] thee and teacheth thee." That is to say: "All the health and life of the sacraments, all the virtue and grace of my word, all the goodness that is ordained by holy church to thee, I it am." (60:25-32.313)

Julian understands that the preaching and teaching of the church, the spiritual food of the "sweet sacraments" that sustain us, the holiness and grace of the Word of God in Scripture, the many blessings that flow from the communal life of the church—all are the extended "nursing" of our mother Christ. And while an earthly mother may give her child milk from her breast, our tender mother Jesus actually leads us *into* his blessed breast through his open side, where he reveals "part of the godhead and the joys of heaven, with ghostly certainty of endless bliss" (60:35 36.313). Julian is convinced that the word "mother" can only truly be applied to Christ, "who is true mother of life and of all" (60:39–41.313).

> In Julian's time, it was believed that the mother's blood (that had previously nurtured the fetus *in utero*) was transformed into milk by the act of nursing. Julian draws the parallel of a nursing mother and Christ feeding us with his precious body and blood in Eucharist and with all the other sacraments. The pelican that pierces its own breast to feed its young with its blood became a poignant symbol of Christ on the cross.

Julian knows well from her own maternal experience that as the child grows older, the mother "changes her werking, but not her love. And when it is more fully grown, she allows it to be chastised to break down its vices, to make the child able to receive virtues and grace" (60:47-49.315). Julian is certain that it is the Lord who does all this work (and disciplining!) "through them by whom it is done" (60:50.315); that is, parents, relatives, teachers, and counselors. Julian also knows that in addition to caring for the physical needs of the child, a good mother must also attend to its spiritual needs, what she terms our "ghostly forthbringing" (61:1.315). In this, our mother Christ uses the utmost tenderness and care:

> He kindles our understanding, he prepares our ways, he eases our conscience, he comforts our soul, he enlightens our heart, and gives us partial knowing and loving of his blissful godhead . . . and makes us love all that he loves for the sake

of his love, and to be well satisfied with him and with all his werks. (61:3-8.315)

Julian attributes every aspect of our spiritual growth to Christ's tender care for our soul. Our best response is to be malleable, teachable, and fully attentive to the promptings of the Spirit. But when we act in ways that harm ourselves or others, or when we fall, like Adam, into grievous sin, then we may think we have utterly failed to be faithful to Jesus Christ. As we shall see, Julian felt the terrible sting of remorse because she felt she had betrayed Christ.

And then we, who are not at all wise, think that all we have begun is nothing, but it is not so. Because it is necessary for us to fall, and it is necessary for us to see it. For if we did not fall, we should not know how feeble and how wretched we are in ourselves, nor also we should not so completely know the marvelous love of our creator. For we shall truly see in heaven without end that we have grievously sinned in this life. And notwithstanding this, we shall truly see that we were never hurt in his love, nor were we ever of less value in his sight. And by the trial of this falling we shall have a high and marvelous knowing of love in God without end. For strong and marvelous is that love which may not, nor will not, be broken for trespass. (61:13-23.315-317)

The Prodigal Mother

Once again, Julian reminds us that "sin is behovely" because, by the mercy of God, it can show us our weakness and our sheer unhappiness when we try to rely on ourselves alone. Recognition of this frightening human condition can bring us to sincere repentance and reveal our total dependency on the unconditional love of God. Furthermore, Julian is certain that "even if our earthly mother might suffer her child to perish, our heavenly mother Jesus may never suffer we who are his children to perish" (61:31-32.317). But when we fall, how are we to seek forgiveness? Like a child in distress and dread, Julian envisions us running quickly to our mother Jesus saying, "My kind mother, my gracious mother, my dearworthy mother, have mercy on me. I have made myself foul and unlike to thee, and I may not nor can not amend it but with thy help and grace" (61:40-42.317). For the child "naturally trusts in the love of the mother in *wele* and in woe" (61:46.317).

And he wills that we take ourselves mightily to the faith of holy church, and find there our dearworthy mother in solace and true understanding with the whole blessed community. For one single person may oftentimes be broken, as it seems to the self, but *the whole body of holy church was never broken, nor never shall be without end.* And therefore it is a seker thing, a good and a gracious thing, to will humbly and vehemently to be fastened and united to our mother holy church, who is Christ Jesus. For the flood of mercy that is his dearworthy blood and precious water is plenteous enough to make us fair and clean. The blessed wounds of our savior are open and rejoice to heal us. The sweet, gracious hands of our mother are ready and diligent about us. (61:47-55.317, emphasis added)

In spite of the papal schism, corruption, and scandals occurring in the medieval church, Julian had a strong sense that the true church is not those who bring disgrace upon it, but *Christ himself.* By taking refuge in the grace of God that comes to us in a multitude of ways, especially in the celebration of Eucharist, we are healed and reunited in community to the mystical body of Christ. In every situation, Christ, our mother and our nurse, "has nothing else to do but to attend to the salvation of her child. It is his office to save us, it is his honor to do it, and it is his will that we know it" (61:57-58.317). All our Savior asks for in return is that "we love him sweetly and trust in him meekly and mightily" (61:59.317). Indeed, in the thirteenth revelation, when Christ showed Julian a glimpse of human brokenness, she understood that even in our terrible failures, Christ never ceases to keep us "full sekerly." Now, in the fourteenth revelation, she realizes this is because *Christ is our mother.* He cares for and protects his children no matter what ditch we fall into, and he lifts us out of our degradation by the sheer force of his love. Indeed, this is how Christ saves—by so completely knitting and *oneing* us to himself that we become who we were originally created to be: the image and likeness of God.

> And from this sweet, beautiful werking he shall never cease nor stop, until all his dearworthy children are born and brought forth. And that he shewed when he gave the understanding of the ghostly thirst: that is, the love-longing that shall last till domesday. (63:19-22.321)

A JULIAN GEM

And I understood no higher stature in this life than childhood, in feebleness and failing of might and of intellect, until the time that our gracious mother has brought us up to our father's bliss. And there shall it truly be made known to us, his meaning in the sweet words where he says: "Alle shalle be wele, and thou shalt see it thyself that alle manner of thing shalle be wele." (63:36-40.321)

Julian's Own Motherhood

Whether by accident or intention, Julian completes her detailed discussion of Christ's motherhood by identifying herself as a mother in union with all mothers. She expresses the hope that in heaven, "the bliss of *our motherhood* in Christ" might begin anew in "the joys of our father God; which new beginning shall last without end, ever newly beginning" (63:40-42.321, emphasis added). In this statement, she reveals herself as one of the mothers who, like Christ, has nurtured, protected, taught, forgiven, and loved unconditionally. She understands further "that all his blessed children who have come out of him by nature shall be brought again into him by grace" (63:43-44.321).

▶ ▶ ▶ THE FIFTEENTH REVELATION ◀ ◀ ◀

Patience, Betrayal, and Healing

In a confessional moment, Julian admits that before her visions began, she had often had a great longing to be delivered from this life of suffering and woe. "And this made me mourn and earnestly long, and also because of my own wretchedness, sloth and weariness, I did not like to live and to travail as it was my duty to do" (64:1-7.323). In other words, Julian frequently felt weary of life and worn out by her daily struggles. She may also have suffered from bouts of melancholy and even depression that made her unwilling to work and pray as she knew she ought to do. But the Lord answered her:

> "Suddenly thou shalt be taken from all thy pain, from all thy disease, from all thy distress, and from all thy woe. And thou shalt come up above, and thou shalt have me for thy reward, and thou shalt be filled with joy and bliss. And thou shalt never more have any manner of pain, nor any manner of sickness, nor any manner of displeasure, nor wanting of will, but ever joy and bliss without end. Why should it then aggrieve thee to suffer [be patient] awhile, since it is my will and for my honor?" (64:10-15.323)

By Christ's answer, Julian was not only comforted; she was taught the inestimable value of the virtue of *patience* in waiting for God to release us from our present suffering. She realizes that if we knew the moment of our death, we would not need to exercise any patience. But since we do not know "the day nor the hour" (Mt 25:13), it is greatly profitable to the soul to live as if it were "ever at the point of being taken. For all this life and suffering that we have here is but a point, and when we are taken suddenly out of pain into bliss, then pain shall be nought" (64:21-23.325). Julian strongly encourages us to "overpass" our present sufferings and emotional upheavals, and contemplate instead the eternal joys that are being prepared for us in heaven. She is certain that:

> It is God's will that we understand his behestes and his comforting as comprehensively and as mightily as we may take them. And also he wills that we take our abidings and our distresses as lightly as we may take them, and set them at nought. For the more lightly that we take them, and the less price that we set on them for love, the less pain shall we have in the feeling of them, and the more thanks and reward shall we have for them. (64:49-54.327)

A JULIAN GEM

And thus I understood that any man or woman who willingly chooses God in this lifetime for love, he may be seker that he is loved without end, with endless love that werks in him that grace [of choosing God]. For God wills we recollect this trustfully, that we are as seker in hope of the bliss of heaven while we are here as we shall be in sekernesse when we are there. And ever the more pleasure and joy that we take in this sekernesse, with reverence and humility, the more it delights him. (65:1-6.327)

Julian perceived that Christ wanted her to be bound to him in love "as if he had done everything that he has done solely for me. And thus should every soul think in relation to his lover" (65:14-15.329). Indeed, she insists that all the revelations were shown to make us all love our Lord and take the greatest delight in him, and fear nothing but displeasing him. If we do, no temptation or evil or suffering can possibly overwhelm us. "For it is his will that we know that all the might of our enemy is locked in our friend's hand"

(65:19-20.329). Here Julian concludes her reflections on the fifteen revelations (with one more still to come):

> Now have I told you of fifteen shewings, as God vouchsafed to minister them to my mind, renewed by illuminations and inspirations, I hope from the same spirit who shewed them all. Of which fifteen shewings the first began early in the morning, about the hour of four, and it lasted—shewing by procession, very beautifully and seriously, each following the other—till it was none [3 p.m.] of the day or past. (65:29-33.329)

Pain and Doubt

Julian writes that the final and sixteenth revelation took place during the night that followed, and it was the "conclusion and confirmation to all the fifteen" (66:2-3.331). However, before she relates it to us, she must confess her own "feebleness, wretchedness, and blindness" (66:4.331). She explains that following the fifteenth revelation she saw no more visions. She even felt that she would recover from her illness and live longer. She reminds us that from the very beginning through the end of the fifteen *shewings* (about eleven hours), she had experienced no physical pain at all. Then, however, the pain returned:

> And anon my sickness came again; first in my head, with a sound and a din; and suddenly all my body was filled with sickness just as it was before, and I was as barren and as dry as if I had never had but a little comfort, and like a wretch I mourned and heaved for feeling of my bodily pains and for the failing of comfort, ghostly and bodily. (66:7-11.331)

How easily we can identify with Julian on this point. Physical pain has an inordinate capacity to disrupt our spiritual equilibrium. In the most self-incriminating terms, Julian describes in detail what happened:

Then a religious person came to me and asked me how I fared, and I said I had raved today. And he laughed loud and heartily. And I said: "The cross that stood before my face, it seemed to me that it bled heavily." And with this word, the person that I spoke to grew all serious and marveled, and anon I was sorely ashamed and stunned because of my recklessness. And I thought: "This man takes seriously the least word that I might say, who saw no more thereof [but what I told him]." (66:12-17.331)

It is shocking indeed to read this confession after the extraordinary visions, locutions, and realizations Julian had been granted from Christ on the cross. Because of her acute physical pain, Julian momentarily doubted and even *denied* her revelations to a total stranger, calling them "ravings"—like those of a madwoman. At first, the friar laughed at her description of herself as a raving lunatic. Then, when she told him that she had seen the crucifix bleeding heavily, he became full of wonder. His look of reverence struck Julian to the heart. She realized that the friar—who had not seen anything of what she had seen—took her seriously. He *believed* her. And she didn't believe God!

Immediately, Julian became very ashamed at the sin of doubt she had committed, and wanted to confess to the friar. But she felt she couldn't because she thought, "How can a priest believe me? I did not believe our lord God" (66:20.333). Nevertheless, she was insistent that she really *did* believe that she had seen Christ on the cross and was committed to believing her revelations for the rest of her life.

But like a fool I let it pass from my mind. Ah, lo I, wretch! This was a great sin and a great unkindness, that I, because of the folly of feeling a little bodily pain, so unwisely abandoned for the time the comfort of all this blessed shewing of our lord

God. Here you may see what I am of myself. But herein would our courteous lord not leave me. And I lay still till night, trusting in his mercy, and then I began to sleep. (66:22-28.333)

The Lord took pity on her and eased her pain sufficiently to allow her to fall into a deep sleep.

Julian's Nightmare

Julian's sense of guilt and betrayal played out in her subconscious mind, producing a nightmare of biblical proportions. She felt herself being choked to death by a skeletal *fiende*. Like the medieval frescoes of devils she must have seen painted on the walls of churches, his faced burned red and hellish, with big black freckles like soot on hot tiles in front of the fireplace. His hair was also flaming red, hanging down in locks on either side of his face. His look and grin were diabolical, his teeth too white and too large. His body was grossly disfigured, and his rough hands were like animal paws. She was being strangled in a satanic death grip. Julian insisted that this *shewing* was *not* a vision like the others (which appeared while she was awake), but rather a nightmare. Yet even within her nightmare, she felt confident that the Lord would protect her.

And in all this time I trusted to be saved and protected by the mercy of God. And our courteous lord gave me grace to wake, and I barely had my life. The people who were with me beheld me and wet my temples, and my heart began to be comforted. (67:9-12.333)

Soon after, Julian smelled a foul stench coming in at the door, producing intense heat. She was terrified there was a fire in the house and they would all be burned to death. She asked if anyone else smelled the smoke. But none did. She cried "Blessed be God!" and gave thanks that it was not a real fire, but rather her own guilty projection of "the fiende that had come to torment me" (67:16-17.335). Then she took refuge in everything that the Lord had shown her on that day, along with the faith of holy church (for she saw both revelations as being one). "And anon, all vanished away, and I was brought to great rest and peace, without sickness of body or dread of conscience" (67:20-21.335).

▶ ▶ ▶ **THE SIXTEENTH REVELATION** ◀ ◀ ◀

Christ in the Soul

At some point during that night, as Julian lay awake, she received the final revelation:

> And then our good lord opened my ghostly eye and shewed me my soul in the middle of my heart. I saw the soul as large as if it were an endless citadel, and also as if it were a blissful kingdom, and by the conditions that I saw therein I understood that it is a worshipfulle city. In the middle of that city sits our lord Jesus, true God and true man: a fair person and of large stature, highest bishop, most solemn king, most honorable lord. And I saw him solemnly clothed in honors. He sits exactly in the middle of the soul in peace and rest, and he rules and governs heaven and earth and all that is. (68:1-8.335)

The sixteenth revelation was a sublime mystical experience of Christ in glory (with recognizable allusions to Rev 21:2-7). However, Julian saw Jesus not in a far-off "heavenly" place, but dwelling within her own soul in the middle of her own heart. In deep contemplation, her soul expanded to become a citadel or castle, like that which stood atop the hill in Norwich. The city surrounding the castle was worshipful, holy, and pleasing to God. There, Jesus Christ, true God and man, sat in the very middle of the city within the citadel (that is, her soul) as the highest bishop, solemn king, and most honorable lord. As in the parable, the Lord sat in peace and rest to rule and govern all creation with mercy and love.

Julian became convinced by this interior vision that "the place that Jesus takes in our soul he shall never leave it without end, as to my sight, for in us is his homeliest home and his endless dwelling" (68:12-13.337). This is because Christ took the greatest delight in the making of a human soul. "For as well as the father might make a creature, and as well as the son knew how to make a creature, so well would the holy ghost ordain that man's soul be made. And so it was done" (68:14 16.337). The Trinity could not have made the human soul any better, any more beautiful, or any nobler than it is. That is why God loves dwelling there.

> But because God made man's soul as beautiful, as good, as precious a creature as he might make it, therefore the blessed trinity is fully pleased without end in the making of man's soul. And God wills that our hearts be mightily raised above the depnesse of the earth and all vain sorrows, and rejoice in him. (68:33-36.337)

A JULIAN GEM

This was a delectable sight and a restful shewing that is without end. And the beholding of this while we are here, it is very pleasant to God, and a very great benefit to us. And the soul that thus beholds, makes itself like to him that it is beheld, and oneth it in rest and in peace by his grace. And this was a singular joy and bliss to me that I saw him sit, for the sekernesse of sitting shewed endless dwelling. (68:37-41.337-339)

In the calm, quiet, "sitting" of the Lord within her soul, Julian took great comfort, for she felt *seker* that the Lord was not going anywhere. Christ will remain sitting on the bare ground of the soul forever. Julian emphasized the importance of "beholding" this "endless dwelling" of Christ in the soul through contemplative prayer, in order that the unfathomable mystery might sink deep into our awareness. Julian was certain that the more often we behold the infinite goodness, compassion, and tenderness of the

Lord of our soul, the more we become like him who is beheld. By his grace, we become united to him in rest and peace.

Thou Shalt Not Be Overcome

As Julian meditated on this blissful affirmation, the Lord gave her "the knowledge that it was truly he that had shewed me all [the revelations] before" (68:42.339). Christ spoke to her one last time, interiorly, without voice or opening of lips, as he had previously:

> "Know it now wele, it was no raving that thou saw today. But take it and believe it, and keep thee therein, and comfort thee therewith, and trust thee thereto, *and thou shalt not be overcome.*" (68:45-47.339, emphasis added)

Julian comments that these words were spoken with the utmost passion by Christ to give her "sekernesse and comfort against all tribulation that may come" (68:55.339). She implies that we too must hold firmly to the truth of all the revelations in times of temptation and trial. However, Julian makes clear that Christ never indicated that our sufferings would suddenly cease. Nor would accidents, illnesses, betrayals, failures, and personal tragedy, for these are all part of our human condition. The Lord meant his words to be understood in a very specific way.

A JULIAN GEM

He did not say, "Thou shalt not be tormented, thou shalt not be wearied, thou shalt not be distressed," but he said, "Thou shalt not be overcome." God wills that we take heed of this word, and that we be ever mighty in seker trust, in wele and woe. For he loves us and delights in us, and so he wills that we love him and take delight in him and mightily trust in him, and alle shalle be wele. (68:55-60.339-341)

What Jesus wanted Julian to know—and by extension, desired all of us to know—is that in spite of our conflicts, weariness, and desperation, he will not allow us to be overcome by evil. Divine light always breaks through our inner darkness, as long as we "mightily trust" that God is at work in absolutely everything we undergo. It is precisely this radical trust that enables us to hope that "alle shalle be wele" even (and most especially) when we cannot possibly see how it could be done.

All Was Finished

"And soon after all was finished, and I saw no more" (68:60.341). With these simple words, Julian ends her account of the sixteen revelations. But the *fiende* returned with new temptations to doubt, with a terrible heat and vile stench, then squabbling with other devils, followed by outright ridicule of those who recite their rosary too loudly, "lacking devout intention and wise diligence, which we owe to God in our prayer" (69:7-8.341). Julian became totally preoccupied with combating these internal demons, and the effort exhausted her. Again, she trusted in the grace of God, setting her eyes on the same crucifix where she had seen Christ, reciting the words of the Lord's passion, and "rehearsing the faith of holy church" (69:13.341)—probably saying the Credo over and over again. This battle for Julian's soul continued throughout the night until the hour of Prime (6 a.m.), when the *fiende* finally left her and only his putrid stench remained. "And I scorned him, and thus was I delivered of him by the virtue of Christ's passion. For 'therewith is the fiende overcome,' as our lord Jesus Christ said before" (69:22-24.343).

Neither Sign nor Token

Julian reflects that the Lord left her with "neither sign nor token" (70:3.343) whereby she might "prove" the truth of her revelations. She received no stigmata (like St. Francis), no relic from the crown of thorns, no remnant of Christ's "dearworthy blood" on her sheets, no change in the crucifix that still stood before her. All was as it had been before.

> But he left with me his own blessed word in true understanding, bidding me full mightily that I should believe it, and so I do. Blessed may he be! I believe that he is our savior who shewed it, and that it is within the faith that he shewed it. And therefore I believe it, forever rejoicing. And thereto I am bound by all his own meaning, with the next words that followed: "Keep thee therein, and comfort thee therewith, and trust thereto." Thus I am bound to keep it in my faith. (70:4-9.343)

A JULIAN GEM

For above the faith is no goodness preserved in this life, as to my sight, and beneath the faith there is no health of soul. But in the faith, there our lord wills we keep ourselves. For we must by his goodness and his own werking keep ourselves in the faith, and by his suffrance of spiritual adversaries, we are tested in the faith and made strong. For if our faith had no enemies it should deserve no reward, by the understanding that I have of our lord's meaning. (70:29-35.345)

For Julian, the firmest and truest confirmation that the revelations had really happened was her *faith* in the word of the Lord within her heart, and the *fact* of her experience: what she saw, what she heard, what she was graced to understand, and how these mystical insights (which she could never have conjured on her own) totally transformed her life. Julian became like the disciples after the resurrection: the only visible "proof" they could give that they had seen the risen Christ was the testimony of their own transformation, from frightened human beings locked in an upper room for fear of the authorities into courageous men and women on fire with the Holy Spirit, now willing to endure any suffering to spread the good news of the risen Lord. Like Mary Magdalene, Julian knew that, in some miraculous way, she too had "seen the Lord" (Jn 20:18).

Once Julian's temptations had passed, she found the greatest joy in the Lord's face that is ever "glad and merry and sweet" in our souls because he beholds our living in great "lovelonging" (71:1-2.345). She became convinced that Christ does not want us to be sad and dour when we pray, but to have a joyous expression because of all he has done and is doing and will do for us. Naturally, there are times in our lives when this seems impossible, but the more we try to maintain a joyous expression, the more Christ himself will "draw the outer countenance to the inner, and make us all at one with him, and each of us with the other in true lasting joy that is Jesus" (71:4-5.345). Strengthened by this incomparable joy, Julian herself became a living witness to what she firmly believed she had "seen" and had been *shewn*. For the rest of her life, under the guidance of the Holy Spirit, she was inspired to contemplate and record the full account of her revelations.

In the Anchorage

Throughout her decades in the anchorage, from the early 1390s to the time of her death, sometime after 1416, Julian continued writing her Long Text, plumbing the deeper meanings of the *shewings* that continued to be revealed to her. In these theological teachings, she shares with her readers the counsel she would have given to those who came to the window of her anchorage seeking comfort, advice, and spiritual direction. She discusses many topics, including the three different facial expressions she saw in Christ on the cross: the face of his passion, the face of his incomparable pity and compassion, and then, his most blissful face. She deals with mortal sin and its destructive power. She explores the knowing of God and of our self—both as we are created and redeemed by grace, and of our self as sinful and feeble. She warns against falling into sloth and despair and about the danger of false humility. She examines four different kinds of dread (or fear) and the nature of God's love, longing, and pity. She offers us ways to avoid sin and the extremes of self-accusation. She teaches us how to bear our suffering in patience, and how to be familiar with the Lord but always courteous and respectful.

Julian sums up four essential things that Christ wants us to know: that he is the ground of our creation and our being; that he protects us and is infinitely merciful toward us even when we sin; that he graciously warns us when we go amiss; and that he always waits for us, without ever changing his expression of love toward us. "For he wills that we be turned and oned to him in love as he is to us" (78:11-12.367). Julian is convinced that if we keep these four realities in mind, we will never sink into despair over our failings because we will always remember that Christ's love for us (like his expression on the cross that never showed any anger or blame) will never, ever change.[29]

> Also our courteous lord, in that same time, he shewed full sekerly and full mightily *the endlessness and the unchangeability* of his love. And also, by his great goodness and his grace inwardly protecting us, he shewed that the love between him and our souls shall never be separated in two without end. And thus in the dread [of sinne], I have matter for humility that saves me from presumption. And in the blessed shewing of love, I have matter of true comfort and joy that saves me from despair. (79:12-18.369, emphasis added)

---

[29]For further discussion of these topics, see Rolf, *Julian's Gospel*, 565-84.

A JULIAN GEM

All this homely shewing of our courteous lord, it is a lovely lesson and a sweet gracious teaching by himself for the comforting of our soul. For he wills that we know, by the sweetness of his homely love, that all that we see or feel, within or without, which is contrary to this [lesson], that it is of the enemy, and not of God. (79:19-23.369)

Julian also describes three noble gifts God has given us in this life by which God is worshiped and we are "profited, protected, and saved"; namely, our natural reason, the common teaching of the church, and the "inward gracious werking of the holy ghost" (80:1-4.371). She states that "God is the ground of our natural reason, and God is the teaching of holy church, and God is the holy ghost" (80:4-5.371). She thinks of these great gifts "as if it were an A.B.C.—that is to say, that we may have a little knowing, of which we shall have fullness in heaven. And that is in order to profit us" (80:9-10.371).

She reiterates her deep conviction that Jesus alone became human and "Christ alone did all the great werks that belong to our salvation, and none but he" (80:11-13.371). Christ dwells in us while we are here, rules and governs us, and brings us into his own blessedness. This he does to such an extent that, "if there was no one else on earth but one, he should be with that one all alone, till he had brought it up to his blessedness" (80:16-17.371). For all that God does for us, Julian affirms that the greatest honor we can give to God is that "we live gladly and merrily for his love even in our penance" (81:13-14.373). He knows only too well that our lives here on earth are full of discord and suffering, but he wills that we set our hearts on the transcending of whatever causes us pain in order to move "from the pain that we feel into the bliss that we trust" (81:22.373).

Life, Love, and Light

Over the years, Julian had an additional illumination about three characteristics of God, which were shown in all the revelations: life, love, and light. By life, she understood God's "marvelous homeliness" or intimacy in the very ground of our being; by love, God's "gentle courtesy" and unceasing care for souls; and by light, God's "eternal being," which never changes in its attitude toward us (83:4-5.377). She also marveled at the fact that our faculty of reason functions *within* God and that it "is the highest gift that we have received, and it is grounded in nature" (83:9-10.377). She further realized that, in addition to the gift of reason, we have been given the most precious gift of faith:

> Our faith is a light, naturally coming from our endless day that is our father, God; in which light our mother, Christ, and our good lord, the holy ghost, lead us in this mortal life. . . . And at the end of woe, suddenly our eye shall be opened, and in clearness of sight our light shall be full, which light is God our maker, father and holy ghost in Christ Jesus our savior. Thus I saw and understood that our faith is our light in our night, which light is God, our endless day. (83:11-13, 17-20.377)

For Julian, the deep source of both our faith *and* our light is none other than divine love, which continually pours itself out to us in the exact measure that we need, and that we can bear to receive, at any given moment. This pure, spiritual love that flows to us from God, which Julian calls "charity," keeps us firm in our faith and in hope; and faith and hope lead to ever greater charity. This charity is never a selfish love, which would seek its own good. On the contrary, charity loves God, and loves itself in God, and loves all that God loves, solely *for the sake of God*. Echoing St. Paul, she concludes: "And at the end alle shalle be charity" (84:7.377).

Julian reflected that in spite of our simplicity and our blindness, our courteous Lord constantly beholds us and enjoys doing his will in us, though we know not how. She counsels us once more that the thing that pleases Christ Jesus most is to *believe* that he enjoys working out our salvation and to "rejoice with him and in him" (85:4.379). Julian attests that in the same way we shall truly be in the bliss of God in heaven, thanking and praising God, likewise, in the foresight of God, have we *always* been "loved and known in his endless purpose from without beginning, in which eternal love he created us" (85:6-7.379). In other words, God sees us now as we shall be then. Moreover, when the final judgment is given, we shall discover in God the hidden reason for everything that has happened in our lives, and how truly we have been loved. Finally, we will understand how God has saved us.

> And then shall none of us be moved to say in any thing: "Lord, *if* it had been thus, it would have been well." But we shall all say with one voice: "Lord, blessed may thou be, because it *is* thus, it is well. And now we see truly that every thing is done as it was thine ordinance to do, before any thing was made." (85:10-13.379, emphasis added)

Not yet Performed

As Julian comes to the end of her Long Text, she declares: "This book is begun by God's gift and his grace, but it is not yet performed, as to my sight" (86:1-2.379). She may have been hinting that, because of the prevailing censorship and fear of condemnation, her book could not be copied or published. Or perhaps she meant that the revelations had not yet been "performed" (in the sense of being fully "enacted") by her *evencristens* for whom she had written it. She begs her readers to "pray together" out of love for God's own working, always "thanking, trusting, rejoicing"

(86:2-3.379). She feels certain that it was our Lord's intention to have this revelation of divine love "known more than it is" (86:6-7.379), though of course, she has no idea how this will happen. She admits that for a long time she wanted to understand *why* the Lord had revealed himself to her in such an extraordinary way. What did it all mean?

A JULIAN GEM

And from the time that it was shown, I desired oftentimes to know what was our lord's meaning. And fifteen years after and more, I was answered in ghostly understanding, saying thus: "What, wouldest thou know thy lord's meaning in this thing [the whole revelation]? Know it well, love was his meaning. Who shewed it to thee? Love. What shewed he to thee? Love. Wherefore shewed he it to thee? For love. Hold thee therein, thou shalt know more of the same. But thou shalt never know therein other without end." Thus was I taught that love is our lord's meaning. (86:11-17.379)

And I saw full sekerly in this and in all [the revelations], that before God made us he loved us, which love was never satiated, nor ever shall be. And in this love he has done all his werks, and in this love he has made all things profitable to us. And in this love our life is everlasting. In our creation, we had a beginning, but the love wherein he made us was in him from without beginning, in which love we have our beginning. And all this shall we see in God without end. *Deo Gracias.* (86:17-22.379-381)

"God is love" (1 Jn 4:8), and the entire story of our salvation is one of divine love. Julian finishes her *Revelations* as she began them, with a reflection on the enclosing Trinity of love: she bears witness to the Creator who formed us out of love, the Savior whose works of love make all things profitable to us, and the Spirit whose love brings us home into eternal life. For Julian, divine love became the answer to all her questions. Over the course of many years, she found the *sekernesse* she had sought all her life: because God is love, "alle shalle be wele."

Here ends the book of the revelations of Julian, anchorite of Norwich, in whose soul may God be pleased. (86:24-25.381)

This ending, from the Paris Codex, is in Latin: *Explicit liber revelationum Juliane anacorite Norwiche, cuius anie propicietur Deus.* It was added later by a scribe.

Digging Deeper into Julian's Themes

Julian's *Revelations* are so full of symbolic language, mystical theology, and multiple layers of meaning that readers may find her text a bit overwhelming at first. There is such a wealth of material to process. To help you navigate your way more easily, I will revisit a few major themes that run throughout the *Revelations* and act like signposts along Julian's visionary journey. I will pose some questions that I hope will spur you to dig deeper into these themes and make your own discoveries. Most importantly, I encourage you to take Julian's themes into quiet reflection so that you may realize their particular relevance for your life. Then, when you have unearthed your own personal treasure from digging into the *depnesse*, you might try writing about your insights, just as Julian did.

Trinitarian Oneing

From the beginning to the end of her *Revelations*, Julian extols trinitarian theology. She may use different terms, but her understanding of Trinity is always that of three distinct and coequal persons in one eternally dynamic substance. Julian teaches that we are *conceived* and *created* by the love of God our Father. Then the mercy of Christ our Mother grants us *rebirth* and the *forgiveness* of all our sins through the outpouring of blood and water on the cross. Finally, we are *sanctified, transformed,* and *brought up into eternal bliss* by the love of the Holy Spirit. Julian also speaks of the eternal trinitarian Godhead "that ever was and is and shall be; all mighty, all wisdom, and all love" (8:7-8.149). For Julian, the Trinity is never an abstract theological dogma but a deeply personal relationship with God as Creator, Protector, and Sanctifier. These three attributes correspond, respectively, with her vision of God as Father, Mother, and everlasting Lover. As we have mentioned, Julian also recognizes three properties of God—life, love, and light—and she sees these different trinitarian properties to be united "in one goodness, into which goodness my reason desires to be oned and to cleave with all its might" (83:5-7.377). She marveled that "our reason is in God" and understood "that it is the highest gift that we have received, and that it is grounded in our substance" (83:8-10.377).

How may we sink our minds into such unfathomable mysteries? Since it is beyond our human ability to "understand" the dogma of one God in three divine persons through a process of reasoning, we must surrender to it in faith. Yet Julian does not imply faith without the aid of reason, but rather writes in the mode of St. Anselm's immortal phrase, "faith in search of understanding."[1] The light of faith must always be seeking a deeper knowledge of God. Faith does not replace understanding. Both faith and the use of our reason are necessary for the fullest love and service of God. At the same time, Julian advises that the more we suspend our tendency to doubt and rest instead within the great abyss of faith, the more easily we may enter into the experience of the Trinity as an

---

[1] Anselm of Canterbury, preface to the *Proslogion*, in *The Prayers and Meditation of Saint Anselm with the Proslogion*, trans. Benedicta Ward (New York: Penguin Books, 1973), 238-39.

all-enveloping divine presence. In addition, the more we take time to reflect on the many attributes of the Trinity, the more we may experience the divine embrace in our worship, our work, and our personal lives. Then the Trinity becomes for us the divine wisdom we seek, the salvation we trust, the love that never fails. The Trinity reveals itself as the indwelling source of all that is, the ground of our being. We experience all of creation arising within a trinitarian mode: the observer, the observed, and the relationship between the two. Our love is understood as trinitarian: I, thou, and the dynamic love that unites.[2]

Throughout her *Revelations*, Julian experienced this mystery of the Trinity in an incarnational way, as Trinity-in-Christ: "For where Jesus appears the blessed trinity is understood, as to my sight" (4:12.135). Hers is a truly *Christocentric* theology. Julian further understood that from the moment of our creation, Christ "knit us and oned us to himself, by which oneing we are kept as clean and as noble as we were made" (58:5-6.307). Indeed, through the presence of Jesus Christ, our soul remains the home of the blessed Trinity. As Julian understood in the sixteenth revelation, "the place that Jesus takes in our soul he shall never leave it without end, as to my sight, for in us is his homeliest home and his endless dwelling" (68:12-18.337). We can never be "left out" of the trinitarian life of God-in-us. In fact, our only existence is within the embrace of the Trinity.

---

[2]St. Augustine drew the analogy between the lover, the beloved, and the love between them as reflective of the three persons of the Trinity: "Now when I, who am asking about this, love anything, there are three things present: I myself, what I love, and love itself. For I cannot love love unless I love a lover; for there is no love where nothing is loved. So there are three things: the lover, the loved and the love." See St. Augustine, "On the Trinity," *Basic Writings of St. Augustine*, vol. 2, ed. Whitney J. Oates (Grand Rapids: Baker, 1992), 790. Augustine also intuited in the rational aspects of the soul a pattern of indwelling Trinity "in the mind, and the knowledge by which it knows itself, and the love by which it loves itself." See St. Augustine, *The Trinity*, trans. Stephen McKenna, in *The Fathers of the Church: A New Translation*, vol. 45 (Washington, DC: The Catholic University of America Press, 1963), 464.

As intimately as Julian experienced the mystical "oneing" of the soul within Trinity, she never suggested that God and the soul are of the *same* substance or essence. She recognized that God alone is divine Creator and we are created. While there is boundless potential for intimacy between divine and human nature, there is never indistinguishable identification.

> And I saw no difference between God and our substance, but as it were all God. And yet my understanding accepted that our substance is in God; that is to say, that God is God and our substance is a creature in God. (54:13-15.297)

Julian also realized that the soul itself is a "created trinity" of reason, memory, and will that has been "known and loved from without beginning, and in the creation, united to the maker, as it was said before" (55:33-35.299). Indeed, Julian saw that because the salvation of Jesus Christ has incorporated us into his mystical body, we are already more spiritual than sensual, more truly "at home" in heaven than on earth.[3]

In studying Julian's trinitarian theology, we must admit that all her exquisite analogies to describe the works of the Trinity pale in comparison with the infinite reality. Julian was most aware of that herself. However, because we humans rely on verbal analogies to lead us to an intimation of the divine, let us reflect on the various terms Julian used for the Trinity and see if they speak to us. Can we think of the Trinity as Creator, Protector, and Sanctifier? As Father, Mother, and Spouse? As power, wisdom, and love? As life, love, and light? Reflecting on the names Julian chose to describe the Trinity may help bring us into deeper union with the indescribable reality they represent: one God in three divine persons.

---

[3]For further discussion, see "Three Aspects of Trinity," in Veronica Mary Rolf, *Julian's Gospel: Illuminating the Life & Revelations of Julian of Norwich* (Maryknoll, NY: Orbis Books, 2013), 516-18. See also Grace M. Jantzen, *Julian of Norwich: Mystic and Theologian* (Eugene, OR: Wipf & Stock, 2005), 110-15.

No Wrath or Blame in God

As we have seen, in the fifth and especially in the fourteenth revelation, Julian repeatedly insisted that she saw no wrath or blame in God. This is because she did not see any wrath or blame in Christ on the cross, as he suffered excruciating pains for the sake of his divine intent to take away our sins. We must ask, in spite of her avowed faithfulness to church teaching, was Julian pushing the limits of orthodoxy here? Not at all. She was reaffirming what Scripture had revealed about the loving-kindness, mercy, loyalty, faithfulness, and unchanging goodness of God, all of which are summed up in the Hebrew word *hesed.* Perhaps Julian had heard the letter of James read in English from the pulpit:

> Do not be deceived, my beloved. Every generous act of giving, with every perfect gift, is from above, coming down from the Father of lights, with whom there is no variation or shadow due to change (Jas 1:16-17).

Insofar as she wrote repeatedly of God's unchanging and unconditional love, Julian remains firmly within orthodox teaching. Nevertheless, she was treading a cultural and ecclesial tightrope. She was challenging the common thinking of her time and the prevalent tone of preaching that depicted God as wrathful, punitive, vengeful, and ready to cast sinners down to hell in fire and brimstone for the smallest sin. Indeed, if one reads English medieval sermons, one is struck by how harsh and unforgiving the language was, not only in condemning the evil of sin but in castigating the sinner. The recurring cycles of plague, bad harvests, famines, cattle disease, even lost battles in the war with France, were all attributed to "the wrath of God" being directed toward sinners. No segment of society, from the richest to the poorest, was exempt from threats of damnation. Women (those "daughters of Eve" who led Adam into the first sin) were deemed especially culpable; it was thought that they continued to deceive men by their lies, hypocrisy, vanity, and seductiveness.

As a much-needed corrective, the *Revelations* showed a God of love, not of wrath. What Julian "saw" in her vision of the passion was a Savior who had nothing but pity and compassion on human beings for the sufferings *we* must endure as a result of our misdeeds. She did not behold a divinity with "mood swings," loving us one minute and putting us on eternal punishment the next. Julian understood that since God is *un*changeable goodness, God does not reject and condemn us when we are guilty of wrongdoing, raining down retribution. On the contrary, it is *we* who, through our sin, bring suffering upon ourselves, our families, our nation, and our world. As we discussed in Julian's ninth revelation, we live in a moral universe in which the law of consequences is continually operative: good deeds produce good rewards and bad deeds receive their punishment (although, as we know only too well, whether in our personal lives or on the world stage, this working out of justice has its own time table). St. Paul strongly affirmed this moral law: "Do not be deceived; God is not mocked, for you reap whatever you sow" (Gal 6:7). All the time, Christ, the Good Shepherd who searches for the lost sheep until he finds it and brings it home, is willing to do *anything* to save us from our own bad choices, even telling Julian: "If I might suffer more, I would suffer more" (22:41-42.197).

Thus we might consider biblical representations of God's wrath to be ancient forms of *literary metaphor* employed by scriptural authors in order to drive home to sinners the enormity of their offenses against divine justice. This language is interpreted by some as projecting onto God the anger and self-blame *we* feel whenever we sin (and even sometimes when we have not sinned, as a manifestation of our low self-esteem). For example, we might assume God must be angry with us because *we* are angry with ourselves and with each other. But as we have seen, Julian maintains that the wrath is all on *our* side: "For I saw no wrath but on humanity's part, and that God forgives in us" (48:5-6.267). She insists that as much as Christ "scorned" the demons and deplores evil, God does not blame us for our sins. Did Christ blame the tax collectors and prostitutes? No, he ate with them. Did he condemn the woman taken in adultery? No, he forgave her, saved her from being stoned to death, and urged her to "Go your way and from now on, do not sin again" (Jn 8:11). Did Jesus turn away when Peter betrayed him? No, he turned *toward* Peter and looked at him with compassion (Lk 22:61). Did Christ lash out at Peter after the resurrection? No, according to the evangelist, Christ asked him three times, "Simon son of John, do you love me?" (Jn 21:15-17). That's all Christ ever wants from us: our love and faithfulness. Furthermore, if God does not blame us for our sinfulness, Julian advises that we must not blame God for our sins *or* our sufferings.

> St. Augustine taught that Scripture uses figures of speech like *lovingkindness*, *mercy*, and *wrathfulness* in order to excite our love and reverent fear of God in ways that symbolic truths set out in abstract fashion cannot. "But no one disputes that it is much more pleasant to learn lessons presented through imagery, and much more rewarding to discover meanings that are won only with difficulty."[4]

Perhaps, like Julian, we heard terrifying sermons growing up that made us feel guilty and condemned by a wrathful God. Maybe we had very strict parents and assumed that the punishments we received from them were fully deserved, even though they seemed

---

[4]St. Augustine, *On Christian Teaching,* trans. R. P. H. Green (Oxford: Oxford University Press, 1997), bk. 2, chaps. VI-VII, 13-14, 33.

extremely harsh at the time. Whether just or not, they may have left us with deep emotional scars. We may have thought of God more as Judge than as Savior; and we obeyed (when we obeyed) out of fear of judgment, rather than out of an eager desire to love and serve. Even as adults, we may find ourselves grappling with Julian's insistence that there is no wrath or blame in God. Perhaps we've been so hard on ourselves for so long. How are we to let go of the pattern of self-blame that has become an integral part of our identity? How are we to experience God as merciful? How can we think of ourselves as being loved unconditionally?

Through prayer and deep reflection, we may gradually reorient our projection of God from an angry, punishing parent to that of a compassionate Savior. Of course, this takes time, determination, and the Holy Spirit's inner working of mercy and grace. Why should it be so difficult? Because, if the truth be told, as much as the idea of divine wrathfulness distances us from God and often turns us against God, it is still "easier" to think of a God who gets angry and punishes us as we deserve, rather than an unconditionally loving God. Such unchanging love seems almost impossible to imagine. To accept the God of love, we must let go of the familiar "me" who feels guilty and unworthy to be loved, the "me" we have always blamed for our misdeeds, the "me" we have lived with all our lives. As Julian writes, we must "nought" ourselves of our negative concept of "self." And that takes time and spiritual work.

Even more importantly, we must consider that an always-loving, ever-forgiving God makes much greater demands on us than might a volatile, angry God (whom we can learn to dismiss). With such a God of absolute love, we must be willing to give all for all. When we fall into human love, we place that love above all other loves. How much more when we fall in love with God! We soon realize we must surrender *unconditionally* to the God of unconditional love. Nothing less is worthy of God: "Not my will but yours be done" (Lk 22:42).

We must dare to reconceive of ourselves as no longer slaves to sin but as God's beloved children. By the power of the Holy Spirit, we must learn to feel intimate and "homely" enough to call God our "Abba!"—just as Christ himself did. Not only that, but because of Christ's redemption of all our sins, we are encouraged to give thanks that we are *already* heirs to God's kingdom (Gal 4:6-7). All this may require a radical readjustment in our day-to-day thinking about God (and ourselves). But that is exactly why it is so imperative that we reflect on Julian's *Revelations*. What Christ showed her in his passion was (and is) not only a liberating release from our age-old obsession with divine wrath and retribution. It was a much-needed *reaffirmation* of God's unconditional love. We may recall Julian's words:

> I saw truthfully that our lord was never wroth nor never shall be. For he is God, he is good, he is truth, he is love, he is peace. And his might, his wisdom, his charity, and his unity do not permit him to be wroth. For I saw truly that it is against the property of his might to be wroth, and against the property of his wisdom, and against the property of his goodness. *God is that goodness that may not be wroth, for God is nothing but goodness.* Our soul is oned to God, unchangeable goodness. *And between God and our soul is neither wrath nor forgiveness in his sight.* For our soul is so abundantly oned to God by his own goodness that between God and our soul may be right nought. (46:24-32.263, emphasis added)

Regarding this revelation, Julian was passionately convinced that "God wills that it be shewn and known" (46:36-37.263). Dare we accept it?

Alle Shalle Be Wele

When Julian heard Christ on the cross assure her that "alle shalle be wele, and alle shalle be wele, and alle manner of thing shalle be wele"

(27:10-11.209), did he mean right away, here and now? You will find that the answer is both no and yes. First, the no. Certainly all was *not* well in Julian's life and her medieval world. All is certainly not well in our own lives and our postmodern world either. Whenever we say "all shall be well" in colloquial speech, to comfort or encourage one another, it is important that we do so with the true intent of the words in mind. Christ did not promise to "fix" what's wrong in our lives and in the world. His words were not meant as an instant panacea for everything that frightens us or those we love. Neither do they offer immediate gratification of all our wants and needs. We cannot be sure we'll land that perfect job, or get that much-needed raise, or be cured of an illness, or fall in love with the perfect person, or marry and have a child, or live happily ever after. Unfortunately, in our broken world, we will not live to see the end of poverty, epidemics, persecutions, wars, or refugees. From our side, Christ's words are prophecy, not yet fulfillment. As long as we live in blindness and ignorance (and cannot see and know God), we will continue to make wrong choices and suffer the consequences, both individually and communally. We will continue to seek what we crave in ways that can injure us and inflict great harm on others. In our human dimension, all will *not* be well any time soon. We still have to face pain, rejection, tragedies, and death.

Yet from the divine perspective, yes these words are already fulfilled. Like the fact of resurrection itself, "alle shalle be wele" signifies that all already *is* well in the ultimate scheme of things. Christ has already conquered sin and death and entered into his glory. Even though we continue to grapple with our demons and temptations, evil has no lasting power over us. We shall "not be overcome" (68:47.339) because Christ has *already* overcome evil. "I have said this to you, so that in me you may have peace. In the world you face persecution. But take courage; I have conquered the world!" (Jn 16:33). According to the faith of the church, in the words of St. Paul, "if we have died with Christ [in baptism], we believe that we will also live with him" (Rom 6:8). This is the ground of our hope.

Nevertheless, because we do not yet have the "spiritual eyes" to see how evil is being overcome, now we must "walk by faith, not by sight" (2 Cor 5:7). Yet our faith is not blindness; it does not mean we walk in the dark. "Faith is a *light*," as Julian wrote. We walk by the light of our faith and by that light we are able to glimpse an entirely different mode of heavenly being where all is already "wele." By the light of faith, we are empowered to hope when everything feels hopeless because we believe that God's goodness "comes down to us, to the lowest part of our need. It revives our soul and brings it into life, and makes it grow in grace and virtue. It is nearest in nature and readiest in grace" (6:25-25.143). Through our faith, we are able to forgive others because we remember the countless times Christ has forgiven us. We are empowered to love those who are not always easy to love because Christ himself loves them from within us. We are graced to bear suffering and intuit the salvific transformation that God is performing even now, in *this* crisis, in *this* tragedy, just as Julian saw Christ transformed in an instant on the cross from agony to glory.

Through this light of faith, we learn to see our daily reality differently, value our blessings more deeply, even anticipate the wonderful surprises the Lord has in store for us. We are able to affirm that the difficult circumstances we experience right now are not the whole story, not even the *true* story of what's really happening. We dare to see "double" in order to experience everything that happens on two levels—human and divine—as Julian did in deciphering the parable of the lord and the servant. Even when confronting great suffering and evil, we perceive with the eyes of faith that there is a divine work in process. It is always and everywhere a work of love, compassion, and radical transformation. We begin to live in the sacred dimension of the Beatitudes, where the poor gain the kingdom, mourners are comforted, the meek inherit the earth, those who hunger and thirst after justice are filled, the merciful receive mercy, the pure in heart see God, the peacemakers are called children of God, and those who are persecuted, reviled, and slandered enjoy a great reward in heaven (Mt 5:1-12). Moreover, we start to view reality not with our own eyes, but through Christ's eyes. Then we can trust that when he looks at humanity, he consumes all that is not good in the fire of his divine love.

Of course, we cannot yet envision our resurrection from death to life, from a life of faith to an eternal life of seeing; nor can we imagine how God will transform the shame we have suffered as a result of our sins into honors in heaven. But we rely on God to do it because of *who God is*. And we count on Christ's mystical presence to be with us every step of the way to heaven. Using five distinct verbal forms, Christ told Julian that he "may" and "can" and "will" and "shall" make all things well, and promised her that she "shall see" herself that all manner of thing shall be well. Furthermore, Julian was granted an intimation of a great deed that will finally make "alle thing wele."

> There is a deed which the blissful trinity shall do in the last day, as to my sight. And what the deed shall be and how it shall be done, is unknown by all creatures who are beneath Christ, and shall be till it shall be done. The goodness and the love of our lord God wills that we know that it shall be. And his might and his wisdom, by the same love, will conceal and hide it from us, what it shall be and how it shall be done. . . . This is the great deed ordained by our lord God from without beginning, treasured and hidden in his blessed breast, known only to himself, by which deed he shall make alle thing wele. For as truly as the blessed trinity made alle thing of nought, right so the same blessed trinity shalle make wele alle that is not wele. (32:19-24, 26-30.223)

What will the great deed be? The final judgment? Universal salvation? A new creation? We have no idea, and since Julian was shown no more than this, she cannot tell us. It must remain mysterious and secret for now:

> And in these same words, I saw a high, marvelous privity, hidden in God, which privity he shall openly make known to us in heaven. In which knowing we shall truly see the reason why he suffered sinne to come, in which sight we shall endlessly have joy. (27:33-36.211)

When we enter into the beatific vision, our minds and hearts will be fully illuminated by divine wisdom and love. In the light of God, we shall know all that truly is and see how the love of God has, indeed, made "alle manner of thing wele."

Julian came to recognize the inevitability that "alle shalle be wele" in the end, precisely because that is how it was "in the beginning" (Jn 1:1). The Word that is the Son of God was always with God and was always God. All things are made in their perfection by God in and through the Word; human beings are fashioned in the image and likeness of the Word who became flesh. Julian understood that the human soul is made by God "of nought. That is to say, it is made, but of nought that is made" (53:33-34.295). While God made the human body from "the slime of the earth," yet in the making of the human soul, "he would take right nought, but made it. . . . And therefore there may nor shall be truly nothing at all between God and man's soul" (53:37-8, 39-40.295). Even though humanity has sinned grievously, through the perfect sacrifice and tireless *werking* of the God/Man, humanity will be brought up again into even greater perfection than in its first creation. Because Christ fell into the ditch of suffering with us and rose from it victorious, Julian firmly believed that we will too. This is a theme that resonates throughout the *Revelations*.

Whenever we speak "alle shalle be wele," can we bear witness that Christ is truly present in this conflict or that tragedy? Can we believe there is meaning in every trial, in every suffering? Can we reassure one another that the ultimate "alle shalle be wele" is being played out *right now* in hidden but very real ways? If we can, something changes radically in our spiritual life. We begin to see with the eyes of faith what we couldn't see happening before. We perceive Christ working in our daily lives in countless ways—both hidden and apparent, and we come to believe that this divine activity is more truly operative and transformative than any human activity could ever be. The two planes of reality—divine and human—no longer seem separated by an unbridgeable chasm. We notice small but unmistakable changes in our personal attitudes, even some marvelous transfigurations. We discover that Christ who is "highest and mightiest, noblest and worthiest" stoops to become "lowest and meekest, homeliest and most courteous" (7:37-38.147-149). This he does in the hidden depths of our soul. We realize we are not alone in our fear, or hurt, or suffering. In fact, we have never been alone. We will never be alone. This realization changes *everything*. Like Julian, we come to trust "mightily" that "alle shalle be wele" because of who God is.

> And thus, this is what he means where he says: "Thou shalt see thyself that alle manner of thing shalle be wele," as if he had said: "Take heed now, faithfully and trustingly, and at the last end thou shalt see truly in fullness of joy." And thus in the same five words before said—"I may make all thing wele" [etc.]—I understand a mighty comfort because of all the deeds of our lord God that are to come. (32:13-18.221-223)

The Parable

May I suggest that you read over the complete parable of the lord and the servant and use Julian's inspired technique of "taking heed" in order to dig deeper into the hidden meaning of parables in your own life? This is especially important to do when things happen that we do not understand, or when we have vivid dreams with significance we cannot decipher. There is a message there, if only we search for it. We may ask ourselves,

Why did that event happen as and when it did in my life?

Why did I feel rejected or hurt or angry?

Why did that great effort I made come to such failure?

What was I meant to learn from the experience? Did I learn it?

Looking back, am I grateful I went through it . . . and survived?

Was it a cause for me to come closer to the Lord—in my desperation, perhaps?

Am I a stronger person because of my suffering?

Can I see that the Lord was working through other people and in my own heart?

Do I have greater compassion for others as a result of what I have endured?

We must believe that nothing happens to us without the possibility of higher meaning—even falling into a ditch. There is always a spiritual gift for us, hidden within the trials and traumas of our lives. But the gift can be uncovered only if we dig deeper and deeper within the silence of our hearts, to get past all the pain that causes so much suffering. So, like Julian, we must keep asking questions, probing to find answers. Eventually, the Lord himself will be the answer, and divine light will reveal the meaning.

The Ground of Being

As she came to understand the parable of the lord and the servant, Julian testifies that the Lord sits on the ground in the center of our being. What is this "ground" to which she refers? For Julian, it is a divine reality out of which all things come into existence and to which they must return. It is a divine awareness that never moves, changes, or alters. This divine awareness enables our human awareness and sustains every moment of our existence. Of course, the ground is not a literal "earthly" ground on which the Lord sits, but the ontological ground of divine knowing and loving that pervades all things, that creates, sustains, forgives, and empowers each one of us. It is from within this sacred ground that the Spirit of Christ cries unceasingly, "Abba, Father." Whether we attend to this ground within us or not, it is always there. In Julian's terminology, it is the substance, or essence, of our very being.

Julian affirms that we cannot truly know ourselves until and unless we come to know God in whom our soul is substantially grounded and "oned."

> And thus I saw full sekerly that it is quicker for us and easier to come to the knowing of God than to know our own soul. For our soul is so deeply grounded in God, and so endlessly treasured, that we may not come to the knowing thereof until we first have knowing of God, who is the maker to whom it is oned. (56:1-5.301)

Yet Julian also understood that we desire to know who *we* are, in our sensual human nature. As mentioned, in Julian's terminology, "sensuality" did not mean the body with its physical and sexual desires but rather the *part of the soul* that produces and perceives everything pertaining to our bodily existence. Our sensuality includes the mind's ability to activate the body and govern its growth, its learning, its health, its maintenance. The soul's sensuality makes us aware of our bodily sensations of pleasure, pain, and suffering. Indeed, for Julian, our awareness of flesh and blood existence is a function not of the body itself but of the sensuality of the soul.

Julian perceived that because God became man in Jesus Christ, God dwells in both our substance and our sensuality as in his own city:

> For I saw full sekerly that our substance is in God. And also I saw that God is in our sensuality. For in the same moment that our soul is made sensual, at the same moment exists the city of God, ordained for him from without beginning; into which city he comes and never shall leave it. For God is never out of the soul, in which he shall dwell blissfully without end. (55:19-24.299)

How can we perceive, like Julian, that God is never "out of the soul"? Julian tells us that we must go into the ground of the soul to cultivate a love-longing for God. At the same time, we must be open to the Lord's work of purification within us. We must remain "in longing and in penance, until the time that we are led so deep into God that we verily and truly know our own soul" (56:22–24.301). Julian is certain that the Lord himself will lead us into a "high depnesse" of contemplative prayer "in the same love with which he made us, and in the same love with which he bought us, by mercy and grace, through the virtue of his blessed passion" (56:24, 25-27.301).

As Christians, we have a profound obligation to become more aware of the presence of Christ's Spirit within our soul. In the sixteenth revelation, Julian took great comfort from the fact that she saw the soul as large as if it were an endless citadel, a blissful kingdom, an honorable city. And she affirmed that in the very middle of that city "sits our lord Jesus, true God and true man" (68.4-5.335). For Julian, Christ's presence is so intimate, he rests on the very *ground* of our being, awaiting our attention. We are invited to sit in quiet meditation, calming the thoughts of our mind and stilling the desires of our heart, so that we might enter into deep silence and thus experience Christ's presence in our soul. Only if we rest in the divine ground can we come to know who God is and who we are. The Spirit continually calls us into this deeper love relationship—"Be still, and know that I am God!" (Ps 46:10). Jesus told us directly: "Come to me, all you that are weary and are carrying heavy burdens, and I will give you rest" (Mt 11:28). But Christ will never force us; it is up to us to choose to spend time with the Lord in the silence of our soul.

I know what you are thinking: *But we lead such busy lives! There are so many demands being made on our time. How can we make a commitment to a daily practice of sitting, waiting, and listening for God?* Every day, like the servant in the parable, we must run off to learn, to create, to work, to serve. But what happens when we trip and fall into a ditch and get mired in the inevitable consequences of a wrong choice? Perhaps like the servant we may experience "seven great pains": our misdeed may bring bodily harm to ourselves and to others; we may feel trapped by a bad decision and unable to find a way out; we may be physically and emotionally debilitated by remorse and guilt; we may become so self-absorbed with our own suffering that we almost forget our love for our Lord; we may be tempted to think we can never rise from this fall or escape this terrible suffering; we may convince ourselves that we're all alone with no one to come to our aid; we may feel so confined by obstacles on every side that we cannot even turn our head to look at our Lord (see 51:20-27.275).

It is then that we realize we have been living on the shaky ground of our conflicting needs and desires instead of on the firm ground of the Spirit of Christ within. It is also then that we understand that the Lord has been waiting for us all along, sitting on the ground of our soul, drawing us out of the muck and mire of our mistakes by his mercy and grace. To be rescued, we have only to become more aware of Christ's presence and redemptive *werking*.

Julian affirms that "God is nearer to us than our own soul" (56:9.301). The ground of our personal being, the center of all our thoughts, desires, and activities, should be, in reality, *God*. "He is the ground of all our whole life in love" (39:36-37.243). And, as Julian was shown, God is also the ground of all our "beseking," our innermost prayer. Our conflicts and troubles arise when we think we are somehow "separate" from our Creator, our Redeemer, our Divine Lover. We can only dispel this illusion of being "cut off" and "on our own" when we take time on a daily basis to rest in God's all-encompassing love in which "we live and move and have our being" (Acts 17:28).

Contemplative Prayer

How are we to develop the ability to experience Christ's presence in the ground of our being? In her teachings on the fourteenth revelation, Julian tells us that it is through the practice of contemplative prayer. It is by entering into silence and stillness that the soul is able to expand beyond the confines of everyday life and realize its boundless capacity for spiritual growth. Gradually, as we learn through meditation to move beyond the myriad thoughts and conflicting emotions that push and pull us in every direction, we begin to drop into a place of peace-filled quiet. It is there in the silence that we may experience the presence of Christ in our soul. It is there that we may be graced with a deeper insight as to how God makes all things well precisely because God is God, and why God can do nothing but make all things well. It is there that we may discover, as Julian did, that Christ "sits exactly in the middle of the soul in peace and rest, and he rules and governs heaven and earth and all that is" (68:7-8.335). As we develop our capacity for contemplative silence, we will be able to let go of our nagging questions, doubts, and fears. Like Julian, we will allow our soul simply to rest, becoming "be-closed" in God.[5]

Love Is the Meaning

Julian's final realization was that "love is the lord's meaning" in all the revelations. Can we believe that love is [and was] the Lord's meaning in our own lives? The meaning of everything that delights us, enriches us, and inspires us, as well as everything that thwarts us, rips open our hearts, and seems to defeat us? Yes, and even that betrays us? Can we convince ourselves that "sin is behovely" because it shows us how much we need divine love to pull us out of the ditch of our misdeeds and to forgive us again and again? Can we hope that "alle shalle be wele" because God loves us and will never be angry with us, blame us, give up on us, or abandon us? We know we will be challenged by both success and failure, by the responsibility of performing good works, and the even tougher responsibility of ac-knowledging our misdeeds. We also know that in Christ we shall not and *cannot* be overcome by evil. This is Christ's promise to us from the Gospels and from his revelations to Julian. That is also Julian's promise to every one of us, her beloved *evencristens*.

---

[5]We will consider the practice of contemplative prayer in more detail in the next chapter.

- 8 -

A Retreat with Julian's *Revelations*

No matter how many times I read the *Revelations*, I am struck anew by Julian's affirmation of the unconditional love and compassion of God that she experienced during her visions of Christ on the cross. Everything she ever wrote was inspired by this experience. There is hardly a page of the eighty-six chapters of her Long text that does not deal with God's love-longing for the soul, and with Christ's infinite pity for our human blindness that leads us into sin and suffering. As we have discussed, in both her Short and Long texts, there is no hint of God rejecting us, even in our misdeeds. On the contrary, it is Christ, the Son of God, who became flesh and fell into the ditch of life with us, who takes on all the blame and negative consequences that could possibly accrue to our sinfulness. God became what we are so that we might become what Christ is.[1]

At times, we may feel compelled to ask, Does God our Father/Mother really love us *that* much, *that* unconditionally? Is Christ's

---

[1]Here, I am paraphrasing the oft-repeated dictum of the ancient and medieval church: "For this is why the Word became man, and the Son of God became the Son of man: so that man, by entering into communion with the Word and thus receiving divine sonship, might become a son of God." St. Irenaeus, *Adversus Haereses*, 3, 19, 1: PG 7/1, 939. "For the Son of God became man so that we might become God." St. Athanasius, *De Incarnatione*, 54, 3: PG 25, 192B. "The only-begotten Son of God, wanting to make us sharers in his divinity, assumed our nature, so that he, made man, might make men gods." St. Thomas Aquinas, *Opusculum*, 57, 1-4.

compassion truly *all*-inclusive? Is the Holy Spirit really present and always *werking* for our benefit in the circumstances of our lives? Are we really meant to become just like Christ? It seems too much to ask, even of God. It overwhelms our ability to comprehend. It feels far too radical. It beggars belief! Yet is it not the message of all the Gospels? Does not our faith tell us that "God so loved the world that he gave his only Son, so that everyone who believes in him may not perish but may have eternal life" (Jn 3:16)? Do we not bear witness that the Word became flesh in order to make us "participants of the divine nature" (2 Pet 1:4)? Perhaps the two biggest questions we have to ask ourselves are: Do we dare believe the full implications of God's unconditional love and mercy? Are we willing to stake our whole lives on it?

To examine these paramount questions more deeply (as well as any others that arise), may I suggest that you take time out for a retreat with Julian's *Revelations*? Such a retreat may begin with a twenty-minute practice each morning and evening, reflecting on a phrase, a sentence, or a paragraph of Julian's text. It may grow into a day's silent retreat in your own home, a weekend getaway retreat in the country, or a communal gathering at a retreat center. It might be an extended week's retreat or an ongoing life retreat. Just imagine what spending prayerful time with *The Revelations of Divine Love* might do to effect spiritual transformation in your life.

For those of you who feel inspired to learn to make a retreat with the *Revelations*, or to lead such a retreat, here are some guidelines from my own years of giving Julian retreats. I have found four things that are absolutely necessary for any type of retreat: silence, reflection, meditative/contemplative prayer, and thanksgiving.

Silence

The most important factor in retreat is to enter into silence. Especially if you are at a retreat house, surrounded by other people. Keeping silence is crucial.

Silence of the eyes. Don't feel the need to make eye contact in passing someone you know (or don't know) in the hallways. No acknowledgment is expected on retreat; in fact, it may distract another person's silence as well as yours. Disconnect your laptop or iPad. Don't check your social networks or the news. Close your eyes and watch your thoughts.

Silence of the ears. Listen only to the retreat leader's talks and/or meditations, the sounds of nature around you, and the still small voice within. Turn off your not-so-smart phones and don't listen to your favorite iTunes. Allow silence to encircle you.

Silence of the lips. Don't feel obliged or inclined to speak to anyone (except, of course in an emergency), even to say please or thank you. Normal courtesies are not expected or desired on retreat. Speak only in prayer.

Silence of the body. Wherever you choose to sit and think, to read or write in your journal, *sit still*. Especially during group presentations or meditations, once you have found a suitable posture, don't fidget or adjust your position, because it will distract your own concentration and that of your neighbor. Slow down your entire body tempo. Even when you walk in the retreat house, or outside in nature, or if you follow a labyrinth, reduce your normal speed to a more reflective pace. Then you can turn all movements into a "walking meditation."

Silence of the mind. Don't chatter to God. Don't make long lists of people for whom you want to pray. God knows your intentions much better than you do. Try not to indulge in fantasies, daydreams, or recycle your worries. Don't rehash old arguments. Don't try to solve problems at home, at school, at work, or with your friends. Place everything in the Lord's care and simply let God love you.

Silence of the heart. Still the pain, the hurt, the struggle that may be weighing on your soul. Seek to replace it with pure love-longing for God. Simply open your heart to receive the Lord's own heart, full of love for you, *personally*. Without thinking about each of them explicitly, be sure to hold the other retreatants gently in your heart, even if you don't know them.

Reflection

The stillness and silence of retreat is a perfect time to practice the ancient Benedictine art of *lectio divina* (divine reading).[2] This process of reflection has four movements, or gradual stages, that take you from reading and meditation to prayer and contemplation. Whether engaging with sacred Scripture or with a holy text like Julian's *Revelations*, *lectio divina* has immense power to bring us into intimate union with Christ—the Word of God—through the words on the page.

1. *Read* one of Julian's revelations in this guidebook, slowly and meditatively. Speak Julian's words—and the Lord's words to Julian—softly to yourself. Choose a particular sentence or phrase that touches you personally. Repeat it several times, reflectively. Allow each word to sink into your heart and resonate there.

2. *Meditate* on the hidden meaning of the passage. As you do, you will naturally commit the passage to memory. Be aware that the Lord is speaking directly to *you* through these words. Remain very quiet and sensitive to the movement of the Holy Spirit within.

---

[2]"The art of spiritual reading as a reflective assimilation of God's Word reaches straight back into the Jewish tradition of meditation: 'Happy are those . . . [whose] delight is in the law of the LORD, and on his law they meditate day and night' (Ps. 1:1-2). Its practice in the Christian church was refined and given special weight by Saint Benedict in the sixth century. In Benedictine tradition, spiritual reading is referred to by its Latin title, *Lectio Divina*. Both Roman Catholics and Protestants owe much of their understanding and practice of scriptural meditation to Benedict. Yet few Protestants are aware that figures like the great Reformer John Calvin and Puritan pastor Richard Baxter advocated a method of reflective meditation with scripture that is directly derived from Benedictine practice. Reformed adaptations of *Lectio* were common among the Puritans." Marjorie J. Thompson, *Soul Feast: An Invitation to the Christian Spiritual Life* (Louisville, KY: John Knox Press, 2005), 24.

3. *Pray* from your heart: a prayer of praise, a word of thanksgiving, a plea for greater understanding, a desire for healing. Whatever arises spontaneously from the reflection, that is your prayer.

4. *Contemplate* the presence of God in your soul. Let go all meditative analysis and verbal prayer, and simply *rest*. "Come to me, all you that are weary and are carrying heavy burdens, and I will give you rest" (Mt 11:28). Allow the infinite love of the Lord to become your rest.

As an additional form of reflection during your retreat, take a walk in a quiet place. Allow the beauties of nature—the sky, the birds, the trees, the flowers, the smell of the air, the colors and shapes of everything—to "speak" to you of God's overwhelming love and maternal care. Take time to notice the smallest details. As you walk, repeat a favorite phrase from Julian's *Revelations* and continue to reflect on its meaning for you.

Be on the lookout for something innocuous—"a little thing the quantity of a hazelnut"—that God creates, protects, and loves, *just like yourself.* It might be something you pick up on the pathway, or find in the woods; it might be a tiny wildflower hiding in the crevice of a wall. Question how this "little thing" embodies your hopes, your struggle, your need, a weight on your heart or a deep-seated fear, your profound sense of gratitude, your longing for greater faith. Perhaps this found object might represent you yourself and the special grace you are seeking from the Lord on your retreat. See the discovery of this humble bit of creation as a gift from God to you. Look at it carefully and hold it lovingly in your hand. You might feel inspired to write a poem about it, sing a song, even dance with it where no one can see you! Keep it safe.

If you feel inspired to write in your retreat diary, do so with the experience of being enclosed in God's love. If you like to draw, make a sketch of your precious object, of nature, of yourself as you are beginning to experience a new self on retreat. Then, at the end of your retreat, offer this "little thing" that represents you to the Lord. Confide yourself in a very special way to Christ's loving care.

Also, throughout your retreat, try to recall and reflect on your own revelations: the *moments*, the *situations*, and the *people* through whom the Lord has revealed and is even now revealing himself to you. Give thanks for them and enclose them in your heart. Make a personal commitment to live by the lights you have received in the past, especially in times of darkness.

If you are leading a retreat focused on Julian's *Revelations*, I suggest asking the retreatants to bring up their personal objects at the last session and present them formally as a symbolic offering to God. Encourage the retreatants to share where they discovered their object (their "hazelnut") and what it represents in their lives. They may also want to read their poems or show their sketches if they are not too personal. I have found that even the most reticent retreatants are eager to tell others how Julian's *Revelations* have become transformative for them. However, for those who wish to remain silent, let them simply place their gift with the others. Some may prefer to sing. Or move in a sacred dance. Any and every expression can be a form of worship and praise to God. This "offering of gifts" in gratitude for Christ's revelations to Julian makes a memorable finale to the retreat.

Meditative/Contemplative Prayer

Making a retreat is the perfect way to learn or to deepen the practice of meditative/contemplative prayer. Here are a few classical instructions to follow on retreat or at home:

- Choose a quiet place, shut the door, and sit down on a chair or a floor cushion with your back as straight as possible. Close your eyes, place your hands gently in your lap, and try to remain perfectly still for the length of the meditation. Take a few minutes to relax whatever tension you feel in your body *from the inside,* without fidgeting or adjusting. Let go of any tightness in your forehead, eyebrows, mouth, neck, shoulders, chest, arms, hands, and so on; but remain alert, vigilant, and aware.

- Follow the whisper of the breath, in and out, like gentle waves lapping on a shore. Try not to "do" anything, even pray. Your primary effort should be to remain still and allow the mind to *become aware* of Who it is who enables every breath. You are breathing God's love, in and out, in and out. Allow the risen Christ to breathe on you the way he breathed on his disciples when they received the Holy Spirit (Jn 20:22).

- As random thoughts and conflicting emotions arise (and they most certainly will), watch them come and let them go, gently, without paying attention to them or grasping onto them or battling them. If you become distracted for a few moments, simply relax, release whatever captured your attention, and refocus on "watching" the breath.

- Once you have become accustomed to these first steps, you may choose a single word or short phrase—known as a *mantra*—that can help you cut through any mental or emotional distractions and stay focused. It might be the name of Jesus, or "Come Holy Spirit," or "Maranatha" (which means "Oh Lord, come!" in Aramaic). Recite the mantra internally, without movement of lips, slowly and rhythmically, along with the breath. It will help keep your mind from wandering off.

> *Maranatha* may have been transliterated from either *marana tha,* which means "Our Lord, come!" (1 Cor 16:22) or *maran atha,* which affirms that "our Lord *has* come." It is both a plea for divine help and an act of faith.

- Start with short sessions—perhaps only ten or fifteen minutes— until it feels natural to meditate like this for twenty minutes. Then establish a daily pattern in which you try to meditate for at least twenty minutes every morning and every evening, no matter what else may be happening in your life. If you miss a session, be patient with yourself. Such a regular practice takes time to develop. Gradually, you will gain consistency and look forward to your meditations. Then retreat becomes a special time when you may be able to intensify your practice, adding more sessions during the day, allowing them to become a little longer as your concentration and ease increase. Your commitment to this practice of contemplative prayer will allow Christ greater freedom to work within you, planting virtuous seeds in your soul that will grow and bear fruit, although you do "not know how" (Mk 4:27).

Eventually, over a long period of time and regular practice, you will "drop" more easily into deeper stillness and mental awareness. You will be able to surrender your life and all your loves into God's care with greater trust. Then whenever you are in crisis or you have a big decision to make, you will more naturally be drawn into the ground of your being, where Christ waits for you to help, forgive, heal, and guide. Then you may be *seker* that whatever choice you make, and whatever happens as a result of that choice, it is God's will for you.

Perhaps you are wondering how this practice of contemplative prayer differs from mindfulness meditation, or the meditation you might do in a yoga class, or any other popular method of calming the mind. The difference lies in its orientation: you are not meditating simply to relax, or to gain mental clarity, or to develop sharper concentration skills (though all these things will indeed come naturally with the practice). The goal is much greater: You are meditating to *experience the presence of God* in the depths of your soul. You are seeking to become more aware of God, the source of all light, truth, and life, so that you might experience the Trinity intimately as Julian did. As we have discussed, this theme of "seeking" and "seeing" runs throughout Julian's text. She encourages us to keep seeking even when we are "in travail," during times of trouble or great labor. We must not give up seeking God's presence through meditation when we struggle with temptation or discouragement. It is then that we most need to rest in God in silent prayer.

Julian assures us that the divinity will reveal itself in due course. We shall "see" him and "behold" him in ever deeper contemplation. "And the clearness of finding is because of his special grace when it is his will" (10:59-60.161). She adds that "the seeking with faith, hope and charity pleases our lord, and the finding pleases the soul, and fulfills it with joy" (10:60-62.161). She reiterates that the soul "that only fastens itself onto God with true trust, either in seeking or in beholding," gives God "the most worshippe that he may do" (10:68-69.161).

> And the beholding of this while we are here, it is very pleasant to God, and a very great benefit to us. And the soul that thus beholds, *makes itself like to him that it is beheld*, and oneth it in rest and in peace by his grace. And this was a singular joy and bliss to me that I saw him sit, for the sekernesse of sitting shewed endless dwelling. (68:37-41.337-339, emphasis added)

Julian is certain that, during a lifetime of seeking and seeing, the soul becomes more and more like the one it contemplates: Christ the Lord, the ground of our being. Is this not reason enough to meditate every day?[3]

---

[3]For more information on the practice of Christian meditation and contemplative prayer, see the World Community for Christian Meditation, www.wccm.org.

Thanksgiving

At some point in the depths of retreat, we may feel overwhelmed by the realization of God's love. For this we must give continual thanks in and through everything we do: "Rejoice always, pray without ceasing, give thanks in all circumstances; for this is the will of God in Christ Jesus for you" (1Thess 5:16-18). Of course, it is comparatively easy to give thanks for all the good and pleasant things in our lives; it is much harder to give thanks for what makes us suffer, what thwarts our plans or causes great hurt. But these too are worthy of thanks, for they teach and strengthen us in ways we will not understand for a long time, perhaps not until the great deed is revealed to us. Sometimes the roadblocks, whether people or circumstances, force us to turn in a different direction. Our failures too can become sources of self-knowledge. And if we get up after every fall, we only grow more resilient, more determined in our resolve. For all this, we give thanks.

There is also another, more unusual aspect to our practice of thanksgiving. Remember the astounding moment in Julian's sixth revelation when she heard the Lord thank *her* for her service and her "travail": that is, both her work and her sufferings? Can you even imagine such a thing? While on retreat, why not allow God to thank *you* for all the ways in which you have tried to serve him during your life, every good deed you have ever done, everyone you have ever loved, every suffering or loss you have endured. In the silence of meditation, imagine Christ saying to you: "Well done, good and faithful servant" (Mt 25:21 NIV). Let your deepest self be loved and appreciated and, yes, *thanked* by God, even as Julian was.

Final Prayer

There is no better way to end a retreat with Julian or a daily meditation practice, than with her own prayer for God to be our "all in all":

God, of thy goodness give me thyself. For thou art enough to me, and I may ask nothing that is less that may be full worshippe to thee. And if I ask anything that is less, ever will I be wanting. But only in thee do I have all. (5:31-33.141)

.

For Further Exploration

Selected Primary Sources for Julian's *Revelations*, Arranged by Date

Revelations of Divine Love: Recorded by Julian, Anchoress at Norwich, Anno Domini, 1373. Edited by Grace Warrack. London: Methuen & Co., 1901.

Comfortable Words for Christ's Lovers. Edited and translated by Dundas Harford. London: H. H. Allenson, 1911.

Revelations of Divine Love, Shewed to a Devout Ankress, by Name Julian of Norwich. Translated by Roger Hudleston. London: Burns, Oates, and Washbourne, 1927; 2nd ed. 1952.

"*A Critical Edition of the Revelations of Julian of Norwich (1542–1416), Prepared from All the Known Manuscripts with Introduction, Notes and Select Glossary*." Edited by Francis Reynold. PhD thesis. Leeds University, 1956.

A Shewing of God's Love: The Shorter Version of Sixteen Revelations by Julian of Norwich. Edited by Anna Maria Reynolds. London: Sheed & Ward, 1958.

A Revelation of Love. The Long Text, British Library, MS Sloane 2499 (S1). Edited by Marian Glasscoe. Exeter Medieval English Texts. Exeter, UK: University of Exeter Press, 1976, rev. ed. 1986.

Julian of Norwich's Revelations of Divine Love: The Shorter Version Edited from BL Add. MS 37790. Middle English Texts 8. Edited by Frances Beer. Heidelberg, Germany: Carl Winter Universitätsverlag, 1978.

A Book of Showings to the Anchoress Julian of Norwich. Vols. 1–2. Studies and Texts 35. Edited by Edmund Colledge and James Walsh. Toronto: Pontifical Institute of Mediaeval Studies, 1978.

Julian of Norwich: Showings. Classics of Western Spirituality. Translated and edited by Edmund Colledge and James Walsh. New York: Paulist Press, 1978.

The Shewings of Julian of Norwich. Edited by Georgia Ronan Crampton. Western Michigan University TEAMS Middle English Texts Series. Kalamazoo, MI: Medieval Institute Publications, 1994.

Julian of Norwich: Revelations of Divine Love. Translated by Elizabeth Spearing. London: Penguin Books, 1998.

Julian of Norwich: Showing of Love. Edited by Anna Maria Reynolds and Julia Bolton Holloway. Biblioteche e archive 8. Florence, Italy: Sisme, Edizioni del Galluzzo, 2001.

Julian of Norwich: Showing of Love. Edited by Julia Bolton Holloway. London: Darton, Longman & Todd, 2003.

The Showings of Julian of Norwich. Edited by Denise Nowakowski Baker. New York: W. W. Norton, 2005.

The Writings of Julian of Norwich, A Vision Showed to a Devout Woman and *A Revelation of Love.* Edited by Nicholas Watson and Jacqueline Jenkins. University Park: Pennsylvania State University Press, 2006.

The Complete Julian of Norwich. Edited and translated by John-Julian Swanson. Brewster, MA: Paraclete Press, 2009.

Julian of Norwich: Revelations of Divine Love, A New Translation. Edited and translated by Barry Windeatt. Oxford: Oxford World Classics, 2015.

Other Primary Sources of Theological and Historical Interest, Arranged Alphabetically

The Ancrene Riwle. Edited and translated by James Morton. London: Camden Society, 1853.

An Anthology of Christian Mysticism. Edited by Harvey D. Egan. Collegeville, MN: The Liturgical Press, 1996.

The Augustine Catechism: The Enchiridion on Faith, Hope and Love. Translated by Bruce Harbert. Hyde Park, NY: New City Press, 1999.

The Book of Margery Kempe. Edited by Barry Windeatt. New York: Longman, 2000.

The Chastising of God's Children and the Treatise of Perfection of the Sons of God, by Jan van Ruusbroec. Edited by Joyce Bazire and Eric Colledge. Oxford: Oxford University Press, 1957.

The Cloud of Unknowing and the Book of Privy Counseling. Edited by William Johnston. New York: Image Books, Doubleday, 1973.

The Corpus Christi Play of the English Middle Ages. Edited by R. T. Davies. Metuchen, NJ: Rowman and Littlefield, 1972.

The Holy Bible (in the Earliest English Versions Made from the Latin Vulgate by John Wycliffe and His Followers). 4 vols. Edited by Josiah Forshall and Sir Frederic Madden. Oxford: Oxford University Press, 1850; reprint, New York: AMS Press, 1982.

Latin Sermon Collections from Later Medieval England; Orthodox Preaching in the Age of Wyclif. Edited and translated by Siegfried Wenzel. Cambridge: Cambridge University Press, 2005.

The Lay Folks' Mass Book or Manner of Hearing Mass. Edited by Thomas Frederick Simmons. London: Trübner & Co., 1879.

The Luttrell Psalter: A Facsimile with Accompanying Commentary. Edited by Michelle P. Brown. London: Folio Society & British Library, 2006.

The Mediaeval Mystics of England. Edited by Edmund Colledge. New York: Scribner, 1961.

A Medieval Garner: Human Documents from the Four Centuries Preceding the Reformation. Edited and translated by George Gordon Coulton. London: Archibald Constable & Co, 1910.

Meditations on the Life of Christ: An Illustrated Manuscript of the Fourteenth Century. Edited by Isa Ragusa and Rosalie B. Green. Translated by Isa Ragusa. Princeton, NJ: Princeton University Press, 1961.

The Mirror of Life of Blessed Jesus Christ, by Nicholas Love. Edited with Introduction, Notes, and Glossary by Michael G. Sargent. Exeter, UK: University of Exeter Press, 2004.

The N-Town Plays. Edited by Douglas Sugano. Published for TEAMS in Association with the University of Rochester. Middle English Texts Series. Kalamazoo, MI: Medieval Institute Publications, 2007.

The Prayers and Meditations of Saint Anselm with the Proslogion. Translated by Benedicta Ward. New York: Penguin Books, 1973.

Preaching in the Age of Chaucer, Selected Sermons in Translation. Edited and translated by Siegfried Wenzel. Washington, D.C.: The Catholic University of America Press, 2008.

The Prymer or Lay Folks' Prayer Book. Edited by Henry Littlehales. London: Early English Text Society, 1895.

The Sarum Missal in English. Translated by Frederick E. Warren. London: The De La More Press, 1906.

The Scale (or Ladder) of Perfection, by Walter Hilton. Scotts Valley, CA: CreateSpace, 2010.

The Select English Works of John Wycliffe. Vol. 3. Edited by T. Arnold. Oxford: Clarendon Press, 1871.

The Trinity, by St. Augustine. Translated by Edmund Hill. Hyde Park, NY: New City Press, 1991.

Women's Lives in Medieval Europe, A Sourcebook. Edited by Emilie Amt. New York: Routledge, 1993.

The York Cycle of Mystery Plays: A Complete Version. Edited by J. S. Purvis. London: SPCK, 1957.

Selected Secondary Sources for Advanced Study

Aers, David, and Lynn Staley. *Powers of the Holy: Religions, Politics, and Gender in Late Medieval English Culture.* University Park: Pennsylvania State University Press, 1996.

Allchin, A. M., et al. *Julian of Norwich: Four Studies to Commemorate the Sixth Centenary of the Revelations of Divine Love.* Oxford: Fairacres, SLG Press, 2001.

Aston, Margaret. *Lollards and Reformers: Images and Literacy in Late Medieval Religion.* London: Hambledon Press, 1984.

Baker, Denise Nowakowski. *Julian of Norwich's Showings: From Vision to Book.* Princeton, NJ: Princeton University Press, 1997.

Barbet, Pierre. *A Doctor at Calvary.* Fort Collins, CO: Roman Catholic Books, 1953.

Bauerschmidt, Frederick Christian. *Julian of Norwich and the Mystical Body Politic of Christ.* Notre Dame, IN: University of Notre Dame Press, 1999.

Beer, Frances. *Women and Mystical Experience in the Middle Ages.* Rochester, NY: University of Rochester Press, 1992.

Bynum, Caroline Walker. *Holy Feast and Holy Fast.* Berkeley: University of California Press, 1987.

———. *Jesus as Mother: Studies in the Spirituality of the High Middle Ages.* Berkeley: University of California Press, 1982.

Cammack, M. M. *John Wyclif and the English Bible.* New York: American Tract Society, 1938.

Coleman, T. W. *English Mystics of the Fourteenth Century.* Westport, CT: Greenwood, 1971.

Coulton, George Gordon. *The Medieval Village.* New York: Dover Publications, 1989.

———. *Studies in Medieval Thought.* New York: T. Nelson and Sons, 1940.

Deanesly, Margaret. *A History of the Medieval Church 590–1500.* London: Methuen, 1925, repr. 1972.

———. *The Lollard Bible.* Cambridge: Cambridge University Press, 1920.

Duffy, Eamon. *The Stripping of the Altars.* 1992. New Haven, CT: Yale University Press, 2005.

Erickson, Millard J. *Christian Theology.* 2nd ed. Grand Rapids: Baker, 1998.

Evans, Gillian R. *Augustine on Evil.* Cambridge: Cambridge University Press, 1982.

Finucane, Ronald C. *Miracles and Pilgrims: Popular Beliefs in Medieval England.* London: Dent, 1977.

Foley, George C. *Anselm's Theory of the Atonement.* New York: Longmans, Green and Co., 1909.

Ford, Judy Ann. *John Mirk's 'Festial': Orthodoxy, Lollardy and the Common People in Fourteenth-Century England.* Cambridge: D. S. Brewer, 2006.

French, Katherine L. *The People of the Parish: Community Life in a Late Medieval English Diocese.* Philadelphia: University of Pennsylvania Press, 2000.

———. *The Good Women of the Parish: Gender and Religion After the Black Death.* Philadelphia: University of Pennsylvania Press, 2008.

Gies, Frances, and Joseph Gies. *Marriage and the Family in the Middle Ages.* New York: Harper & Row, 1987.

———. *Life in a Medieval City.* 1969. Reprint, New York: Harper Perennial, 1981.

Glasscoe, Marion. *English Medieval Mystics: Games of Faith.* Edited by C. Brewer and N. H. Keeble. New York: Longman Medieval and Renaissance Library, 1993.

Hide, Kerrie. *Gifted Origins to Graced Fulfillment: The Soteriology of Julian of Norwich.* Collegeville, MN: Liturgical Press, 2001.

Hodgson, Geraldine Emma. *English Mystics.* London: A. R. Mowbray, 1923.

Horrox, Rosemary. *The Black Death.* Manchester: Manchester University Press, 1994.

Huizinga, Johan. *The Waning of the Middle Ages.* New York: Dover Publications, 1999.

Inge, William Ralph. *Studies of English Mystics: St. Margaret's Lectures.* London: J. Murray, 1906.

Jantzen, Grace M. *Julian of Norwich: Mystic and Theologian.* Eugene, OR: Wipf & Stock, 2005.

———. *Power, Gender and Christian Mysticism.* Cambridge: Cambridge University Press, 1995.

Jessop, Augustus. *The Coming of the Friars and Other Historic Essays, Including "The Black Death in East Anglia."* London: T. F. Unwin, 1884.

Keen, Maurice. *English Society in the Later Middle Ages, 1348–1500.* New York: Penguin Books, 1990.

Knowles, David, with Dimitri Obolensky. *The Middle Ages.* London: Darton, Longman & Todd, 1969.

———. *The English Mystical Tradition.* New York: Harper, 1965.

———. *The English Mystics.* London: Burns, Oates, and Washbourne, 1927.

Kroll, Jerome, and Bernard Bachrach. *The Mystic Mind.* New York: Routledge, 2006.

La Verdiere, Eugene. *The Eucharist in the New Testament and the Early Church.* Collegeville, MN: Liturgical Press, 1996.

Leech, Kenneth, and Benedicta Ward. *Julian Reconsidered*. Fairacres Publications 106. Oxford: SLG Press, 2001.

Llewelyn, Robert, ed. *Julian: Woman of our Day*. London: Darton, Longman & Todd, 1985.

McAvoy, Liz Herbert. *Authority and the Female Body*. New York: D. S. Brewer, 2004.

McEntire, Sandra J., and Joyce E. Salisbury, eds. *Julian of Norwich: A Book of Essays*. Garland Medieval Casebook 21. New York: Garland Reference Library of the Humanities, Taylor and Francis, 1998.

McGinn, Bernard. *The Varieties of Vernacular Mysticism (1350–1550)*. New York: Herder & Herder, 2012.

McKisack, May. *The Fourteenth Century, 1307–1399*. New York: Oxford University Press, 1991.

Merton, Thomas. *Conjectures of a Guilty Bystander*. New York: Image, Doubleday, 1966.

———. *Seeds of Destruction*. New York: Farrar, Straus, and Giroux, 1964.

Mohl, Ruth. *The Three Estates in Medieval and Renaissance Literature*. New York: Frederick Ungar Publishing Co., 1962.

Molinari, Paolo. *Julian of Norwich: The Teaching of a Fourteenth-Century English Mystic*. New York: Arden Library, 1979.

Nuth, Joan M. *Wisdom's Daughter: The Theology of Julian of Norwich*. New York: Crossroad, 1991.

Oliva, Marilyn. *The Convent and the Community in Late Medieval England: Female Monasteries in the Diocese of Norwich, 1350–1540*. Rochester, NY: Boydell Press, 1998.

Olson, Linda, and Kathryn Kerby-Fulton, eds. *Voices in Dialogue: Reading Women in the Middle Ages*. Notre Dame, IN: University of Notre Dame Press, 2005.

Orme, Nicholas. *English Schools in the Middle Ages*. London: Methuen and Co., 1973.

———. *Medieval Children*. New Haven, CT: Yale University Press, 2001.

Owst, G. R. *Preaching in Medieval England: An Introduction to Sermon Manuscripts of the Period c. 1350–1450*. New York: Russell & Russell, 1965.

————. *Literature and Pulpit in Medieval England.* Cambridge: Cambridge University Press, 1933.

Palliser, Margaret Ann. *Christ, Our Mother of Mercy: Divine Mercy and Compassion in the Theology of the Shewings of Julian of Norwich.* Berlin: Walter de Gruyter, 1992.

Pantin, W. A. *The English Church in the Fourteenth Century.* Cambridge: Cambridge University Press, 1955.

Pelikan, Jaroslav. *The Growth of Medieval Theology 600–1300.* Vol. 3 of *The Christian Tradition: A History of the Development of Doctrine,* Chicago: University of Chicago Press, 1978.

Pelphrey, Brant. *Christ Our Mother: Julian of Norwich.* Wilmington, DE: M. Glazier, 1989.

————. *Love Was His Meaning: The Theology and Mysticism of Julian of Norwich.* Salzburg: Institut für Anglistik und Amerikanistik, Universität Salzburg, 1982.

Peters, Edward, ed. *Heresy and Authority in Medieval Europe.* Philadelphia: University of Pennsylvania Press, 1980.

Power, Eileen. *Medieval English Nunneries, c. 1275–1535.* Cambridge: Cambridge University Press, 1922.

Prosser, Eleanor. *Drama and Religion in the English Mystery Plays.* Palo Alto, CA: Stanford University Press, 1961.

Renevey, Denis, and Christiania Whitehead, eds. *Writing Religious Women: Female Spiritual and Textual Practices in Late Medieval England.* Toronto: University of Toronto Press, 2000.

Riehle, Wolfgang. *The Middle English Mystics.* Translated by Bernard Standring. London: Routledge & Kegan Paul, 1981.

Rolf, Veronica Mary. *Julian's Gospel: Illuminating the Life & Revelations of Julian of Norwich.* Maryknoll, NY: Orbis Books, 2013.

Shahar, Shulamith. *Childhood in the Middle Ages.* London: Routledge, 1992.

————. *The Fourth Estate: A History of Women in the Middle Ages.* London: Routledge, 2007.

Spencer, H. Leith. *English Preaching in the Late Middle Ages.* Oxford: Clarendon Press, 1993.

Sullivan, Edward, OP. *The Image of God: The Doctrine of St. Augustine and Its Influence*. Dubuque, IA: Priory Press, 1963.

Tanner, Norman P. *The Church in Late Medieval Norwich 1370–1532*. Studies and Texts 66. Toronto: Pontifical Institute of Mediaeval Studies, 1984.

Thompson, Marjorie J. *Soul Feast: An Invitation to The Christian Spiritual Life*. Louisville, KY: John Knox Press, 2005.

Thouless, Robert Henry. *The Lady Julian: A Psychological Study*. London: SPCK, Sheldon Press, 1924.

Tuchman, Barbara W. *A Distant Mirror: The Calamitous 14th Century*. New York: Random House, 1978.

Turner, Denys. *Julian of Norwich: Theologian*. New Haven, CT: Yale University Press, 2013.

Ullmann, Walter. *A Short History of the Papacy in the Middle Ages*. 2nd edition. London: Routledge, 2003.

Underhill, Evelyn. *Mysticism: A Study in Nature and Development of Spiritual Consciousness*. London: Methuen, 1911.

———. *The Essentials of Mysticism and Other Essays*. London: Dent, 1920.

Vinogradoff, Paul. *Villainage in England*. Oxford: Clarendon Press, 1892.

Ward, Jennifer C. *Women in England in the Middle Ages*. London: Hambledon Continuum, 2006.

Watson, Nicholas. "Censorship and Cultural Change in Late Medieval England: Vernacular Theology, the Oxford Translation Debate, and Arundel's Constitution of 1409." *Speculum* 70 (1995): 822-64.

Williams, George Hunston. *Anselm: Communion and Atonement*. Saint Louis, MO: Concordia, 1960.

Wood, Diana. *Women and Religion in Medieval England*. Oxford: Oxbow Books, 2003.

Woolf, Rosemary. *The English Mystery Plays*. Berkeley: University of California Press, 1980.

Workman, Herbert Brook. *John Wyclif: A Study of the English Medieval Church*. 2 vols. Eugene, OR: Wipf & Stock Publishers, 2001.

Young, Karl. *The Drama of the Medieval Church*, vol. 1. Oxford: Clarendon Press, 1962.

Ziegler, Philip. *The Black Death*. New York: Harper Perennial, 2009.

General Index

Scripture Index

About the Author

Veronica Mary Rolf is an independent scholar educated at Columbia University, an academic lecturer, a former Broadway actress, professional playwright, and a Master Teacher of Dramatic Arts in New York, London, Buenos Aires, and Berkeley. She is the author of *Julian's Gospel: Illuminating the Life & Revelations of Julian of Norwich* (Orbis Books), which won a First Place Catholic Press Association Book Award, the Nautilus Gold Medal Book Award for Spirituality, and the National Indie "Excellence" Book Award for Religion/Non-Fiction.

After a long career playing leading roles on Broadway, in classical theatre, and on television, Veronica was appointed as the first actress in the Affiliate Artist program, sponsored by the National Endowment for the Arts. In this capacity, she performed her One Woman Shows as a goodwill ambassador throughout the United States. As a dramatist, she has seen her plays produced on the New York stage and on television. She was also the founding Artistic

Director of *The Center for Creative Collaboration, Inc.* in New York City, dedicated to helping at-risk youth through the arts, the marketplace, and the community.

Veronica has been married for over forty years to the actor/director Frederick Rolf. Their son, David, is a senior technology executive and their daughter, Eva Natanya, PhD, is a scholar of comparative religion. Currently, Veronica lectures on the history and theology of Christian mysticism and leads contemplative retreats throughout the San Francisco Bay area. She is a certified teacher of meditation, affiliated with the World Community for Christian Meditation. She manages the Julian of Norwich Group on Facebook and writes about spiritual topics on two websites: www.juliansvoice.com and www.veronicamaryrolf.com.

The Explorer's Guide Series

An Explorer's Guide to Karl Barth
978-0-8308-5137-9

An Explorer's Guide to Julian of Norwich
978-0-8308-5088-4